OECD Digital Government Studies

Digital Government in Chile – Improving Public Service Design and Delivery

Please cite this publication as:
OECD (2020), *Digital Government in Chile – Improving Public Service Design and Delivery*, OECD Digital Government Studies, OECD Publishing, Paris, *https://doi.org/10.1787/b94582e8-en*.

ISBN 978-92-64-75860-5 (print)
ISBN 978-92-64-40417-5 (pdf)

OECD Digital Government Studies
ISSN 2413-1954 (print)
ISSN 2413-1962 (online)

Photo credits: Cover © Fundación Imagen de Chile.

Corrigenda to publications may be found on line at: *www.oecd.org/about/publishing/corrigenda.htm*.

Foreword

The way that services are designed and delivered shapes citizens' experience of government. Although digital transformation has affected all aspects of daily life and replaced many of our human interactions, government must continue to ensure that the services it provides are accessible to all. This means doing more than simply migrating analogue processes to the Internet.

"Digital government" efforts involve recognising the role of design in meeting citizen needs across all channels, unlocking the benefits of digitalisation while protecting those who rely on face-to-face transactions. Such design needs to be complemented by developing and embedding practical resources and technical support to help teams avoid the constraints and expense of transforming services one at a time. This 'Government as a Platform' approach can scale transformation from the most high profile and capable through to the least developed and equipped government services at every level of provision, including local.

Digital Government in Chile – A strategy for public service design and delivery presents a conceptual framework to help countries explore how to make best use of the opportunities of the digital age in designing and delivering services. Through recognising the context that shapes the design and delivery of services, establishing the necessary leadership and vision to develop a design-led culture, and ensuring access to practical enablers, governments can increase their ability to improve outcomes, efficiency and measures of citizen satisfaction and well-being. The report analyses the situation in Chile and provides a series of recommendations for considering the future role of ChileAtiende, a branded multichannel network for accessing government services throughout Chile. Ultimately, they contribute towards Chile's goal of bringing the State closer to citizens through simpler, more efficient and transparent government.

As requested by the Ministry General Secretariat of the Presidency (*Ministerio Secretaría General de la Presidencia*, MINSEGPRES) and the Ministry of Finance (*Ministerio de Hacienda*), this is the fourth piece of work prepared for Chile by the OECD's Digital Government and Data Unit in recent years and reflects a concerted effort to create the conditions for digital government to thrive. In 2016's *Digital Government in Chile – Strengthening the Institutional and Governance Framework* the OECD advised Chile how to build solid foundations and 2019's *Digital Government in Chile – A Strategy to Enable Digital Transformation* developed this further. Third, and also in 2019, the practicalities of digital identity as an enabler for services, and in particular Chile's own ClaveÚnica were the subject of *Digital Government in Chile – Digital Identity*. They provide a path for digital government in Chile to support efforts at delivering better lives for citizens. These foundations are essential to the discussions of this report in facilitating the design and delivery of services that respond to the needs of the public.

The report is based on the *OECD Recommendation of the Council on Digital Government Strategies* and contributes to the global policy debate on the challenges and opportunities of digitalisation across different policy areas and all of society. This is part of the Going Digital Project, which is the OECD flagship initiative designed to address this important policy issue.

The report was declassified for publication by the Public Governance Committee on May 7, 2020.

Acknowledgements

Digital Government in Chile – A strategy for improving public service design and delivery was prepared by the OECD Directorate for Public Governance (GOV), under the leadership of its Acting Director, Janos Bertok.

The report was produced by GOV's Open and Innovative Government Division (OIG). It benefitted from the strategic orientation and revisions of Barbara-Chiara Ubaldi, Head of the Digital Government and Open Data Unit.

The report was drafted by Benjamin Welby, Digital Government Policy Analyst (OIG). The author is grateful to Felipe González-Zapata, Digital Government Policy Analyst (OIG), in the finalisation of the report and to Liv Gaunt (OIG) for editorial support.

The analysis contained within the report would not have been possible without the valuable support and knowledge provided by the following public officials from OECD countries who acted as peers during the peer review mission to Santiago in January 2019:

Ignacia Orellana, Service Designer, Government Digital Service, United Kingdom

Paulo Vale, Project Manager and Policy Officer – Digital Transformation, Administrative Modernisation Agency, Portugal

The project itself would not have been possible without the support of the Ministry General Secretariat of the Presidency (*Ministerio Secretaría General de la Presidencia*, MINSEGPRES) and its Digital Government Division, the Ministry of Finance (*Ministerio de Hacienda*) and its Modernisation Secretariat, the Social Security Institute (*Instituto de Previsión Social*, IPS) and ChileAtiende. In turn, this agenda is strongly supported by the Inter-American Development Bank and the OECD is grateful for the contributions of Pedro Farias, Modernization of the state principal specialist at the IDB.

The report benefitted from the expertise of the OECD Working Party of Senior Digital Government Officials (E-Leaders) and in particular that of the United Kingdom in its leadership of the Thematic Group on Service Design and Delivery.

Finally, the Secretariat would like to acknowledge the contributions of Francisco Rodríguez, Head of the Digital Government Division of the Chilean Ministry General Secretariat of the Presidency, Kareen Schramm, Policy and Digital Government Research Co-ordinator of the same institution, and Amaya Fraile, Head of the Modernisation Secretariat of the Chilean Ministry of Finance. The OECD would also like to thank Randall Ledermann, Paula Manque, María Isabel Silva, and Francisco Carrillo for their contributions and without whom this project would not have been possible.

Table of contents

Figures

Boxes

Executive Summary

The promises of politicians, the goals of manifestos and the hopes of electorates set high expectations for our relationship with government. Where these abstract ideals are translated into public service delivery, the design of those exchanges determine our experience of government.

It is hard to imagine a world without the service layer of government administration. Historically, public sector organisations have handled those interactions manually, on paper, and with varying degrees of bureaucratic headache. These processes result from decisions about how government is to be consumed. Some are inevitable, given the structure of government, while others reflect economic, social, political or technological context; all contribute to a citizen's experience in relation to the state.

OECD countries are increasingly acknowledging the importance of design in the quality of the services government delivers. The OECD's *Digital Government in Chile* series reflects Chile's ongoing commitment to deliver a government that maximises the opportunities of the digital age to reduce the burden and cost of interactions between citizen and state while increasing satisfaction, effectiveness and, especially, trust. *Digital Government in Chile – A strategy for public service design and delivery* focuses on the citizen experience of government and specifically the service delivery network ChileAtiende with a concern that digital progress and its benefits should not exclude those who rely on face-to-face interactions.

Although ChileAtiende is effectively branded, enjoys political backing and reports high satisfaction levels amongst the public, it provides access for only a fraction of overall transactions. Scaling the design and delivery of high-quality services throughout Chile will require greater delivery co-ordination and co-operation among public sector organisations as well as establishing and encouraging a service design culture supported by the necessary enablers.

This report considers the intersection of Chile's digital, telephone and physical service channels, and identifies the importance of ensuring the same service experience for all users, in all contexts, through all channels. To make the physical, offline and digital elements of a service work together in meeting user needs, **service design** is critical. It provides the basis for service delivery and the resulting experience for the public by:

- understanding a user's journey from their first attempt at solving a problem, through to final resolution (from end to end),
- addressing citizen-facing experiences and back-office processes as a single continuum rather than two separate models (from external to internal, and vice versa), and
- creating consistency of access and experience across and among all channels (omni-channel).

The report draws on the experience of OECD member countries, the Working Party of Senior Digital Government Officials (E-Leaders) and its Thematic Group on Service Design and Delivery, and analysed through Digital Government Reviews of member and non-member countries. It establishes a three part conceptual framework for thinking about service design and delivery that underpins the analysis of Chile and ChileAtiende in order to enhance the design, and delivery, of public services:

1. **The context that surrounds designing and delivering services** in terms of legacy approaches and the nature of political support, amongst other factors.
2. **The philosophy expressed through the leadership and vision for designing services** that meet the needs of the public and in the behaviours of delivery that support that design.
3. **The practical enablers that need to be built, enhanced and supported** so teams can avoid the constraints and costs of transforming services one at a time, and instead design and deliver high-quality services at scale, from the most high profile and capable through to the least developed and equipped at every level, including local. This 'Government as a Platform' approach includes sharing best practices and guidelines; governance, spending and assurance; digital inclusion; common components and tools (such as digital identity, notifications and payments); data governance and its application for public value; and public sector talent and capabilities.

This report provides specific policy recommendations (summarised below and developed further in the Assessments & Recommendations chapter) to unlock the opportunity for rethinking cross-government service design and delivery beyond ChileAtiende in order to achieve the ambition of the 2019 Digital Transformation Law to digitalise 100% of public services by 2025.

Key policy recommendations

- Define a clear cross-government strategy and coherent action plan for the government of Chile to establish and nurture a design culture that places users at its heart, in order to respond to their needs across all channels and throughout the policy and delivery lifecycle.
- Enable Chilean public sector organisations to understand the needs of the public in order to be proactive in finding solutions to the problems that cause the most pain and the highest costs.
- Ensure a joined-up and simple-to-navigate experience of government with brand clarity for all interactions between government and its stakeholders, whether citizen, business or visitor.
- Commit to an inclusive experience of government services that builds on Chile's expertise in offline service provision to ensure those services are understood:
  - from when someone first attempts to solve a problem through to its resolution (from end to end)
  - on a continuum between citizen experience and back-office process (external to internal)
  - across any and all of the channels involved (omni-channel).
- Secure cross-government political and administrative support for a holistic service design and delivery agenda ensuring 'Government as a Platform' enablers to scale transformation from the most high profile through to the 'long tail' of government services, including:
  - a clear data strategy
  - guiding principles and guidelines
  - the necessary human capital
  - technical and practical support to common components such as digital identity and payments
- Establish clear organisational responsibilities to provide coherent governance and effective leadership between:
  - the Ministry General Secretariat of the Presidency (*Ministerio Secretaría General de la Presidencia*, MINSEGPRES) and its Digital Government Division and LabGob (*Laboratorio de Gobierno)*,
  - the Ministry of Finance (*Ministerio de Hacienda*) and its Modernisation Secretariat,
  - the Social Security Institute (*Instituto de Previsión Social*, IPS) and ChileAtiende, and
  - the Civil Service.

Assessments and Recommendations

This section assesses the context and philosophy of services in Chile, and the enablers to support services. It also presents the recommendations on how to improve service design and delivery.

In recent years, Chile has been working with the OECD to explore the opportunities and potential of digital government approaches to transform the relationship between the citizen and the state and improve the quality of government services. This has involved work to strengthen the governance arrangements for digital government (OECD, 2016[1]), develop a clear strategic vision for the future (OECD, 2019[2]) and consider the role of digital identity (OECD, 2019[3]).

These areas of work are critical for developing the foundations of the digital transformation of the public sector but count for nothing if they are not considering an ambition for delivering better policies and services that transform the lives of citizens and businesses in their interactions with government. This fourth study considers that ambition for Chile to deliver a government that reduces the burden and cost of interactions between citizen and state whilst increasing satisfaction, effectiveness and trust.

Government services need to work effectively and efficiently wherever and whenever citizens and business have need of them. Interactions that would once have taken place in person have increasingly moved towards a dematerialised, online experience. Nevertheless that transition from one channel to another takes place against an existing context in which there are a patchwork of physical channels, often implemented as part of a sectoral one-stop-shop agenda that runs in parallel and in addition to the web presences of each service providing entity.

This study on the design and delivery of services within Chile focuses on the cross-governmental one-stop-shop ChileAtiende, and explores the practical steps and political and institutional changes that would be necessary to deliver a whole of government, cross-Chilean strategy for unifying the citizen experience of interacting with the Chilean state to deliver better outcomes and more effective government. This study is especially timely given the ongoing implementation of the Digital Transformation of the State Law (*Ley de Transformación Digital*) (MINSEGPRES, 2019[4]) which promises to digitalise interactions between Chileans and the government, opening up a unique window of opportunity for rethinking service design and delivery in a coherent and cross-governmental way. For such a strategy to become a common agenda that is supported and understood by the whole of government, the following are needed:

1. A strategic and holistic approach that considers the context, behaviours and enablers for service design and delivery in Chile.
2. Understanding services from the point at which someone first attempts to solve their problem, until its resolution (holistically from end to end rather than within organisational siloes of provision).
3. A commitment to securing the same quality of services and transformed citizen experience across all channels so that they work as one, rather than adopting different solutions for different channels (omni-channel as opposed to multi-channel).
4. A recognition that the public, citizen facing experience exists on a continuum with the way in which public servants in a back office respond to those needs (external to internal).
5. For the concepts of "digital by design", "Government as a Platform" and a "data-driven public sector" to be embedded for accelerating the transformation of the public sector to achieve internal efficiencies, deliver better value to all citizens, and avoid discrimination based on the personal choice of channel.

The context for services in Chile

Since its inception ChileAtiende has had a value proposition of reducing transaction costs for citizens and business in interacting with the government of Chile through a centralised multi-channel service delivery approach. This approach brings benefits to users as they can access multiple services through a single channel; as well as to the government by increasing the efficiency and coherence of service delivery.

ChileAtiende enables institutions to reach more people through increased coverage of face to face transactions as well as its digital platforms and call centre acting as a signpost to services accessed elsewhere. This means that ChileAtiende has the potential to amplify and catalyse the delivery of smaller organisations who do not have the luxury of funding and capacity found in larger organisations. This allows for thinking about and protecting the 'long tail' of government services that would otherwise never receive the focus, or attention, necessary to provide a transformed citizen experience. This may become even more relevant with the entry into force of Chile's Digital Transformation of the State Law (MINSEGPRES, 2019[4]), which recognises the extent to which public services are experienced at the local level and applies to every tier of government.

Outside government the ChileAtiende network of physical locations, website and call centre is an established and well-recognised brand seen by Chilean citizens as delivering a high quality, and valued, experience, albeit handling only 6% of transactions between citizen and staff (Ministerio de Hacienda, 2018[5]). The commitment of staff to meeting the needs of the public and ensuring their satisfaction across each of its channels is striking. It is clear that the physical ChileAtiende locations are not only a source of pride to staff, but responsive to the needs of the public too. The decision by the ChileAtiende and Social Security Institute (*Instituto de Previsión Social*, IPS) team to seek specific innovation funding to reduce and remove barriers for those with particular access has resulted in a welcoming and inclusive atmosphere.

Nevertheless, ChileAtiende does not reflect an omni-channel approach: where the design and architecture of services supports access through any channel, from any device, at any point in a new or existing service journey. Instead, the different channels do not work as one to deliver the same service or quality of service. The piecemeal simplification and digitisation of pockets of government in response to sectoral needs or the priority of a given one-stop-shop has produced bespoke solutions operated on a channel by channel basis. This means services available through the website are the not the same as the call centre and those are not the same as the solutions available to agents in the physical locations or installed on the self-service kiosks. It also means that users cannot reliably predict what services will be available whilst there is an overhead for the ChileAtiende team in maintaining different levels of access through different solutions. Only the team from the Directorate of Labour (*Dirección del Trabajo*, DT) demonstrated a more sophisticated ambition to develop an omni-channel approach.

The focus on physical interactions should be understood through the demand for face to face access in Chile. Providing access to services for those who cannot, or choose not to, use digital and telephone based channels is an important element in any strategy for delivering access to services. Age demographics and cultural expectations are understood as the reasons for limited success in achieving channel shift thus far. Alongside these challenges the service provision landscape in Chile appears to be a factor with the constraints of existing digital identity provision in particular a barrier to the transformation of services.

The most striking feature of that landscape are the myriad organisations providing their own service channels. Indeed, only 6% of transactions between citizen and state take place under the auspices of ChileAtiende (Ministerio de Hacienda, 2018[5]) . Although ChileAtiende exists as a central citizen service delivery channel the coexistence with websites, call centres and physical locations offered by other organisations in the Chilean public sector create additional complexity for citizens, project a fragmented image of government and undermine the success of ChileAtiende.

With each institution wanting to keep their own identity and host their own services this creates multiple locations, telephone numbers and websites, all with their own brand recognition. To the external observer this looks like a confused picture. For citizens however, there is familiarity in accessing the relevant provider and their physical location, call centre or website to meet their specific needs. The current ease with which citizens can visit physical locations to access services provided by the Service of Civil Registration and Identity (Servicio de Registro Civil e Identificación, SRCel), the Internal Revenue Service (Servicio de Impuestos Internos, SII), the National Health Fund (Fondo Nacional de Salud, FONASA) or other agencies is supported by a confidence that those interactions will meet their needs. With no strategic approach to the holistic provision of services across Chile, whether in person or online these channels proliferate and partnerships between different organisations rely on internal relationships rather than following from a clear mandate to deliver a unified experience for citizens.

One of the most important short-term opportunities in the Chilean public sector comes from taking the high service standards of the face to face experience of ChileAtiende and ensuring that it is reflected in the approach taken to any other channel and in the underlying culture of other government service providers. In this way, a set of standards and expectations for the 'front door' to interactions with government can provide a consistently excellent experience. There has been some success in identifying ChileAtiende as the single brand through using the website and call centre as a single entry point to services across government. However, that brand recognition is diminished if it is simply an index signposting to websites or physical locations owned and branded by others, rather than being a genuinely unifying user experience that consolidates government to simplify and streamline life for users.

Longer-term, any strategic vision and commitment to an omni-channel approach of consolidating access to services under a single brand across all channels needs to be complemented by the necessary 'Government as a Platform' resources and enablers. These will support the teams holding responsibility for particular users and their needs to deliver consistently designed services more quickly and effectively. However, the lack of a clear vision for whether ChileAtiende is to become the service delivery brand for government or in establishing a consistent user experience makes it inevitable that other government institutions see ChileAtiende as an extension of IPS rather than a government wide programme.

As a consequence, inclusion in the ChileAtiende digital platforms or call centre is seen as a low cost (or even no cost) way of growing an organisation's own coverage rather than as an endorsement of the ChileAtiende network. Instead of being the prelude to migrate towards consolidated platforms for service delivery, several organisations had the expectation of ChileAtiende adopting their back office systems. Not only does this create challenges for the staff within the ChileAtiende networks in managing a multiplicity of software, it codifies the siloed approach to government delivery and undermines efforts to create an integrated, interoperable approach to services.

Despite the efforts of the Digital Government Division (DGD) within the Ministry General Secretariat of the Presidency (*Ministerio Secretaría General de la Presidencia,* MINSEGPRES), there is still a strong tendency to take an organisation specific approach to designing and delivering public services. This means their development is not built around an understanding of the whole problem facing a user and so there were only limited examples of organisations working together to meet an end to end need. This situation is exacerbated by evidence of drawn out processes to allow bilateral agreements for sharing data internally while the organisation specific approach to training budgets and performance reporting reinforces those siloes.

These challenges mean that the structure and organisation of government is too often taking primacy at the expense of the needs of the public. Nevertheless, where ChileAtiende has built partnerships, particularly with smaller organisations (such as the National Consumer Service *(Servicio Nacional del Consumidor,* SERNAC*)*), it demonstrates the potential of the network to deliver value for citizens in increasing the breadth of access. Indeed, several of the other service delivery networks had successfully developed partnerships with local and regional government. In these cases, the conversation is moving beyond any question of branding or platform ownership to a focus of teams working across governmental boundaries to more efficiently deliver the foundational ambition of better access to higher quality services.

The philosophy of services in Chile

The ambition of better access to higher quality services was at the heart of the ChileAtiende project on its inception. Over the subsequent decade, the prominence of ChileAtiende has ebbed and flowed whilst the service delivery and administrative simplification agendas, coupled to the evolution of technology, have inspired and motivated organisations throughout the Chilean public sector to explore the digitisation of its citizen facing and internal processes and procedures. However, the lack of a service delivery model based on a strategic user-driven approach, with institutional roles, governance mechanisms and a specialised staff to support it means that there remains an e-government era view of deploying front-end or back-office technology as the solution to providing online channels. Chile has yet to fully adopt digital government approaches that consider the entire citizen experience in light of the opportunities provided by data and digital tools to rethink how the public sector works in order to deliver end to end transformation.

Chilean organisations are conscious of the inefficiency and failure demand caused by existing analogue processes and use an analysis of triggers for high demand as the basis for digitising a given service. However, this means that in the case of several potentially high profile transactions, such as that involving criminal records or claiming medical leave, the process was being digitised without a recognition of the potential for revisiting the steps and procedures underlying the delivery of the service and rethinking its design in light of new data or technology opportunities.

In general, organisations were content with the status quo and happy with the incremental digitisation of the next step in the process rather than considering the broader opportunities to improve outcomes for their users. This was not true of every organisation with the team at DT particularly impressive in framing the challenges they faced within a narrative of service design to proactively avoid the effort of either citizen or public servant that reflected the vision being provided by the organisation's senior digital leadership. Overall, it appears that transformation efforts owe more to individual activities within an organisation rather than being coordinated. With the passage of the Digital Transformation of the State Law (MINSEGPRES, 2019[4]), there is a critical window of opportunity for public agencies to reorient service design and delivery towards the needs of their users beyond user experience practices, having ChileAtiende as a suitable platform to channel those services under a common user experience and branding.

One of the barriers to planning the future shape of the service delivery landscape in Chile is the still inconsistent cataloguing of services across government and the lack of a map detailing the flow of data access and re-use between organisations. Although recently a catalogue of services has been officially put in place, further efforts are required to standardise the concepts and data being used in the service delivery domain. Without this it will remain complex for the government to develop a detailed understanding of how different channels, organisations and the services themselves hang together or design the necessary incentives to effect any migration away from the existing situation of multiple brands with their own channels.

This limited cross-government coordination, or agreement over the philosophy underpinning service design and delivery, coupled to an underestimation of the value of unified branding and a single entry point into government information and services (supported by full integration of back end processes, systems and data) means there is confusion about the current and future purpose of ChileAtiende. Government wants more services to come under the umbrella of ChileAtiende and for this service delivery brand to have prominence, but at the same time there is a desire to preserve the channels offered by different organisations and their branding as long as they reflect ChileAtiende's customer service model. This reflects the lack of strategic thinking between service delivery and broader government goals around competitiveness and productivity which are high priorities for the country.

Nevertheless, it is important to recognise that the ambition should not be for a single, consolidated team responsible for delivering all services across government but methods for scaling good service design practice and embedding it as part of the DNA of government. The ChileAtiende network has already proven itself a valuable laboratory for exploring approaches to customer service but to transform the service design and delivery context in Chile will require a mandate to work with the Service Council and the Modernisation Council and Committee to inspire a different model of delivery throughout government (including partnering with DGD, the Government Laboratory (*Laboratorio de Gobierno,* LabGob) and the Modernisation

Secretariat). There is a consequent need to increase the frequency, quality, effectiveness and direction of communications between public institutions and the government to develop the opportunities for achieving the necessary shift in behaviour.

Ultimately, Chile does not have a clearly stated, and commonly accepted, vision for delivering consistently excellent services across all channels that prioritises the needs of the user and which can be accessed through a unified entry point. 2020 provides an opportunity to restate the original ambition and refresh its vision for the next decade of ChileAtiende to inspire a whole of government adoption of that mandate. Through the Digital Transformation of the State Law (MINSEGPRES, 2019[6]), the government is attempting to change its way of doing business in order to increase its efficiency and improve its relationship with citizens. It is, indeed, a significant opportunity to put common standards for service design and delivery at the core of the digital transformation of the State.

Ensuring a shift in the approach of government as a whole involves leadership and governance arrangements at every level: cross-government, in institutions and amongst 'ordinary' staff. At the centre of government, multi-disciplinary thinking is important for developing the strategic future for ChileAtiende. That leadership team needs to be able to cast a vision for an inspiring future for service design and delivery whilst navigating and influencing thinking in this area amongst senior public servants and political appointees. In each organisation, the impact of Director level appointees who understand the opportunity is significant, but it is in the collaboration between organisations where individuals can work together as a network to develop a culture of digital leadership that will propagate different ways of thinking and working. Equally, at an individual level, there need to be ways for talent that already exists in government, regardless of their level of influence or job title, to meet and support like-minded individuals (in a similar way to Chile's Public Sector Innovators Network).

The enablers to support services in Chile

In ChileAtiende, Chile has a ready-made, highly regarded network for providing services to the public. However, to enable it to fulfil its promise it is crucial for Chile to identify, and prioritise, work to support the enablers for digital government and service delivery.

Although the absence of common components addressing payments and notifications constrain the development of new services, the most important building block for Chile to develop is Digital Identity and the accompanying interoperability of underlying data. Its current absence is a barrier to basic channel shift and more effective integration because without a robust solution, digital and telephone based service channels can only provide information and generate new transactional siloes. The new vision for ClaveÚnica offers an approach that it is not simply about identity and therefore unlocks the potential for transforming services by rethinking the nature of interaction between citizen and state rather than just digitising an existing process.

It is encouraging to see a high priority placed on Digital Identity and to see progress on the development of other enabling tools and resources provided by DGD for re-use by teams across the public sector. Making these tools the de facto choice of delivery teams across government will depend on the extent to which further investment is made available. While mandating the use of particular resources is one route to ensuring this takes place, perhaps as part of the spend controls process, DGD would benefit from developing a more mature 'service wrapper' to encourage the adoption of these resources and continue to improve the value they offer. All in all, there several missing steps in terms of security, transparency and governance for ClaveÚnica which need to be considered at the time of rethinking service design and delivery in the country (OECD, 2019[3]).

There is a nascent data-driven culture within the Chilean government. However, in general, public agencies do not want to share data and there are no incentives or mandates to make this happen whilst an interoperability platform for electronic services has been developed in the past it is not widely used with citizens having to provide the same information multiple times. Addressing the issues with the country's data infrastructure is essential but this must come as part of a broader strategic approach to data governance and sharing. It was encouraging to learn that a national data strategy is under development and will draw on the OECD's framework for a data-driven public sector (OECD, 2019[7]) but there is a still a gap for the function of a Chief Data Officer to provide clarity across government about data governance, the application of data and the role of data in building public trust, and its necessary linkage with the service delivery agenda. There has been a good start in using data to understand performance but the challenge remains in applying it throughout the Government Data Value Cycle. It is relevant to ensure this data strategy is developed under a collaborative and participatory approach in order to increase its appropriateness and ownership.

The ongoing evolution of procurement in Chile offers some optimism that this important factor in enabling service transformation will improve over time. However, procurement was identified as being a blocker to some of the ambitions either in terms of its efficiency, dynamism or in the outcomes that it had produced. Long-term contracts with expensive change control processes remain a constraint in terms of designing and developing services that can iterate in response to the needs of users (such as the identity management contract from SRCel).

One of the most encouraging characteristics of the ChileAtiende model is the strength of its customer service culture. Although that culture results in high levels of satisfaction and important efforts to transform the experience of interacting with ChileAtiende it is not the same as a user-driven approach centred on placing the needs of users at the core of the design of underlying services. In some parts of government there was a lack of involvement from stakeholders (whether citizens or public agencies) and a view that users needed to be educated in order to use a service rather than investing in its design. However, in other organisations there were clear efforts to move towards such a user-driven approach and a desire for the centre of government to be more explicit and take a stronger stance in terms of governing and assuring the quality of services. Although DGD is providing certain cross-cutting enablers and LabGob is encouraging the adoption of design and innovation practices, the model by which MINSEGPRES and the Modernization Committee would enforce quality controls or provide common standards to underpin the way services are designed and delivered is less developed.

It was clear that there was a shortfall of the necessary capabilities in order to incorporate more services into ChileAtiende or to take a different approach to their design in the first place. Whilst procurement can provide a vehicle to bringing the necessary talent into government, the most sustainable way to transform the design and delivery of services is embedding an innovation and user-driven design culture across government through the recruitment and training of public servants, an area in which Chile's LabGob is already playing a valuable role. A particularly important group of staff to consider are those who are currently employed throughout the Chilean service delivery networks. As the current landscape involves multiple networks meeting organisation specific needs there are concerns amongst Chilean Trade Unions that a consolidated approach under the ChileAtiende brand would lead to job losses but there are opportunities for retraining this group of people in the skills needed for digital service design and delivery as well as for strengthening existing physical channels to improve quality and efficiency of service.

Recommendations

1. Define a clear cross-government strategy and coherent plan of actions to create and nurture a design culture that places users at its heart and is driven by their needs

- Develop training and reference materials in service design and delivery practices drawing on the experiences of other OECD countries as discussed throughout Chapter 2.

- Develop training and reference materials in customer service drawing on the experience of ChileAtiende and mandate its usage by all other service delivery networks
- Establish a Head of Design role for the government and encourage similar appointments at an institutional level
- Identify existing networks in Chile, such as the coordinators of Digital Transformation, ChileAtiende counterparts, the Protected Middle Class network (*Clase Media Protegida*, CMP) or the network of public innovators, and work with them to manage change and establish a culture of service delivery based on citizen needs.
- Alongside those formal networks encourage policy teams, delivery teams and operational teams to work together by creating communities of practitioners from similar disciplines and fostering service communities of those responding to similar needs. Design appropriate incentive mechanisms and performance objectives that are focused on embracing a service design culture and promote collaboration in design, sharing of data and building common understanding of the needs of shared users and their journeys.
- Use governance tools, such as planning for new public programmes and evaluation of projects to incorporate an expectation for service design based on user needs. This could include making it an explicit requirement in existing evaluation approaches or management improvement policies carried out by the Ministry of Finance Budget Office or the Ministry of Social Development.
- Partner with the Civil Service to define and develop dedicated training on integrated service design within Chilean public agencies.
- Strengthen the collaborative relationship between DGD and LabGob to encourage an innovation culture throughout the Chilean public sector that supports adoption and change management in implementing digital services.

2. Enable public sector organisations to develop an understanding of the needs of the public in order to be proactive in finding solutions to the problems that cause the most pain and the highest costs

- Establish a Head of User Research role for the government and encourage similar appointments at an institutional level
- Strengthen the *Registro Nacional de Trámites* and its integration with other sources of information such as ChileAtiende, the CMP network, and PymesGob among others. Identify all those involved in delivering these services by including detail on the flow of data between institutions and encouraging user research to understand:
  - the end to end experience of accessing them for users
  - the effort and challenges involved in delivering and operating them for teams
  - the associated costs and how to reduce them (in terms of the time it takes, and the efforts involved, for the public and government to completely resolve an issue)
- Establish a unit or role with responsibility for strategically analysing the register of services in order to understand opportunities for rationalising services and defining digitalisation, transformation and adoption strategies as part of the existing governance for service delivery.
- Recognise the methodology for measuring user satisfaction developed by the Modernisation Secretariat as the standard for the Chilean public sector and take active steps to encourage its adoption by those public agencies with significant service delivery responsibilities in order to allow comparative analysis across government.
- Design a user research process to benchmark all existing service delivery channels (digital, telephone, physical) against this performance baseline. Determine what short-term training is needed to bring all citizen experiences into line.

3. Ensure a joined-up and simple-to-navigate experience, with coherent branding, for all interactions between government and businesses, citizens and visitors

- Assign to the inter-institutional coordination committee the task to provide distinct professional leadership for those working in the disciplines of policy and service design, user research, delivery, software engineering, web operations, operational and customer service professionals across government. Ensure resources are available to convene and coordinate cross-government communities of practice, identify best practices and success cases.
- In the mid-term develop Chile's Government as a Platform ecosystem (see Recommendation 6) to equip teams and government suppliers with the necessary resources to meet the needs of users with an omni-channel, self-service experience with a consistent look and feel. This should include:
  - Best practices and guidance materials
  - Business case support for accessing funding, ongoing procurement reform, and the assurance and enforcement of standards
  - Resources to support digital literacy, connectivity and accessibility
  - Common components delivering discrete functionality (such as identity, notifications and payments) as well as more generic design resources forming the basis of a common design system
  - The relevant aspects of the OECD's data-driven public sector model
  - A strategic approach to public sector talent and capabilities.
- As a longer-term ambition set the vision and strategy for ChileAtiende to become the single government service delivery brand for accessing services across multiple channels and with the ultimate intention to consolidate, and rationalise, the Chilean public sector's web and physical presence. Activity associated with designing and delivering those services should remain with those organisations with single, or shared, responsibility for a particular set of needs supported by the ongoing efforts of LabGob to encourage a more Agile, experimental and iterative approach.

4. Commit to an inclusive, omni-channel, end to end experience of government building on Chile's expertise in offline service provision

- Develop a service standard reflecting the omni-channel ambitions of the Chilean public sector. The priority given by Chile to the offline experience of citizens and the importance of face-to-face interactions provides an opportunity to develop a digital by design, rather than digital by default, assurance process that takes into account existing offline processes and the value they provide.
- Establish an assurance process for monitoring the implementation of this standard and include its provisions in business case and performance evaluation processes
- Ensure that the internal experience of working with ChileAtiende to include new services or adopting any 'Government as a Platform' enablers is as easy as possible to facilitate those organisations responsible for the 'long tail' of government services that would otherwise be left as analogue interactions
- Identify services that touch on multiple organisations including across tiers of government. Select at least one to form the basis for a cross-government service community to develop exemplar services. The funding model for this exercise needs to incentivise collaboration and ensure that different parts of government do not end up feeling that they are competing with one another rather than working together. Exemplars should:
  - be citizen-driven: involving the public throughout the design and delivery process to ensure their needs are understood

  - solve an end to end problem: considering the user's journey from the moment they identified a need through to its resolution, regardless of how many organisations and interactions are involved
  - proactively meet needs: rather than being initiated by a user, exemplars should look to anticipate requests and, through integrated access to data, reduce the interactions that are needed
  - take innovative approaches: explore how a policy or service might be reimagined to achieve the desired outcomes through the use of new ideas, technologies or applications of data where appropriate
- Promote digital inclusion efforts to remove and reduce barriers to the adoption of digital services. This should include developing new or strengthening existing strategies for:
  - connectivity throughout the country
  - developing clear standards for accessibility of all services and all channels for those with disabilities
  - working with community groups, voluntary organisations, civil society organisations and municipal governments on initiatives to increase digital literacy
- All face-to-face locations, including ChileAtiende, should become the focus for partnerships to move beyond delivery of services to become hubs for activity around civic participation and digital inclusion and consequently encourage adoption amongst the public.
- Identify opportunities for transparently communicating progress in terms of service design and delivery efforts through blogposts and videos as well as physical workshops and demonstrations within ministries and local communities to stimulate ongoing engagement and participation of all stakeholders

5. Secure cross-government political support for a holistic service design and delivery agenda

- Through the Modernisation Committee secure political capital in support of the service design and delivery agenda and secure a commitment for integration between the big service providers and ChileAtiende.
- Design a governance model for services that includes all the key stakeholders and ensures their ongoing coordination. This should build on the existing role of the Service Council in coordinating ChileAtiende (IPS), CMP network (Ministry of Social Development and Family (*Ministerio de Desarrollo Social y Familia,* MDS)), Ministry General Secretariat of Government (*Ministerio Secretaría General de Gobierno*, SEGEGOB), Ministry of Economy, Development and Tourism (*Ministerio de Economía, Fomento y Turismo de Chile*), DGD and the Civil Service.
- Clarify the institutional responsibility for service design and delivery in Chile and ensure there are sufficient mandate and resources for the lead organisation(s) to execute the ambitions contained in this report, in collaboration with the main public service providers. They need to be able to involve the appropriate actors and identify, publicise and enforce assurance criteria that achieve a focus on proactive service delivery, driven by citizens and tailored to their needs.
- Strengthen the strategic coordination between DGD and LabGob for a coherent and integrated approach towards service design and delivery standards and practices considering both the expansion of the ChileAtiende network and need to implement the Digital Transformation of the State Law (MINSEGPRES, 2019[4]).
- Bring together all those involved in digital leadership networks at least twice a year to be inspired by the service design challenges and opportunities being explored across Chile. Use these as opportunities to invite public sector leaders, especially those with 'non-digital' roles.

6. Secure the availability of enabling 'Government as a Platform' resources

- Take advantage of the Digital Transformation of the State Law (MINSEGPRES, 2019[4]) as an exceptional and strategic opportunity to transform the way services are designed, integrated and delivered to citizens. This means going beyond the digitalisation of public services and UX practices, giving larger attention to embedding cross-sectoral service design and delivery standards and the coherent coordination and integration within the government to satisfy final users' needs.
- Establish the function of a Chief Data Officer for the government and encourage similar appointments at an institutional level.
- As stated in the Digital Transformation Strategy, develop a National Data Strategy in line with the OECD's data-driven government framework to fulfil the ambition of citizens to provide information once only and provide the necessary legal and technological frameworks to ensure digital security.
- Continue the efforts led by DGD to establish interoperability arrangements across the Chilean public sector.
- Prioritise the development and strengthening of ClaveÚnica as the sole mechanism for identity validation, authentication and advance electronic signature within the Chilean public sector, in line with the recommendations provided by the OECD (2019[3]).
- Prioritise the development, ongoing implementation and support for take-up of common components, such as payments and notifications, which can speed up the delivery of digital services informed by user research into the common needs of service teams.
- Invest in the capacity and coordination of DGD and LabGob to lead on the uptake and development of 'Government as a Platform' enabling tools and resources as a service to address concerns and questions of public servants. This needs to involve the following areas of activity:
    - Develop an engagement and 'marketing' function to handle account management for common components and tools with those teams that are using them and that can identify the reasons other teams are choosing not to.
    - Showcase the tools and resources available for use by teams in the public sector and ensure regular communication throughout government to raise awareness of new capabilities
    - Support the product teams to meet user needs well through addressing barriers to adoption and, in particular, making initial onboarding for experimentation very easy and being responsive to support needs.
    - Proving the value of using common resources by having clear value statement about what they offer to a user. Work with service teams using the 'Government as a Platform' ecosystem to analyse the benefit of enabling tools and services. Offer ongoing support to measure impact, produce case studies detailing the cost benefit analysis of adoption, and provide template business cases for teams making the funding requests to support implementation.

7. Governance, roles and the organisational responsibilities required to support and encourage service design in Chile

It is essential that clear responsibilities are established and the relevant roles identified in order to provide coherent governance and effective leadership across government. Where appropriate this should iterate the legal and regulatory framework to provide a formal basis for the following:

- Secure through the Executive Committee for the Modernisation of the State the long-term vision and governance mechanisms for the coherent implementation of service design, delivery and data strategies.

- Establish a permanent strategic coordination body for service design and delivery in Chile, involving relevant stakeholders in the provision of public services in the country, such as DGD, Ministry of Finance (*Ministerio de Hacienda*), IPS, Ministry of Social Development and Family (*Ministerio de Desarrollo Social y Familia*), LabGob and Civil Service. At an operational level, coordination to be carried out by the Service Council with participation from the aforementioned newly established roles of Head of Design, Head of User Research and Chief Data Officer
- MINSEGPRES, Ministry of Finance (*Ministerio de Hacienda*) and IPS should assume responsibility for normalising the service design and delivery agenda by:
    - setting out a clear omni-channel strategy
    - mapping the existing service landscape and identifying the prioritisation criteria by which services are identified for transformation
    - providing the necessary incentives to stimulate coordination
    - disseminating good service design practices
    - funding the delivery of any enablers for collaboration
    - establishing performance indicators to track and audit progress
- DGD to have the mandate for providing practical elements of the service toolkit for design and delivery teams including standards, guidance and design resources for achieving omni-channel services as well as those activities associated with interoperability, identity management and the citizen wallet, payment systems, and data infrastructure and architecture.
- IPS to be responsible for setting clear customer service guidelines and develop appropriate training for interacting with the public through any channel including forums, social media, web chat as well as physical and telephone. In collaboration with DGD and LabGob, coordinate cross-government user research and analysis of the priority needs to meet as well as developing an effective mechanism for evaluating performance across channels.
- LabGob to work closely in partnership with DGD to develop the standards, guidance and design resources and with IPS to support the analysis and understanding of needs through qualitative and quantitative methods including proactive user engagement to gather. Moreover, work with individual institutions to provide assistance in embedding a user-centred and user-driven culture towards designing services.
- Individual institutions are responsible for adopting these design and delivery standards in their services and channels and work towards their inclusion, and perhaps eventual migration, to ChileAtiende. Training in line with the service design and delivery strategy should be prioritised by individual organisations.

References

Ministerio de Hacienda (2018), *Presentación Nueva Institucionalidad ChileAtiende*. [5]

MINSEGPRES (2019), *Estrategia de Transformación Digital del Estado*, Ministerio Secretaría General de la Presidencia. [6]

MINSEGPRES (2019), *Ley 21.180 de Transformación Digital del Estado*, https://www.leychile.cl/Navegar?idNorma=1138479 (accessed on 12 December 2019). [4]

OECD (2019), *Digital Government in Chile – A Strategy to Enable Digital Transformation*, OECD Digital Government Studies, OECD Publishing, Paris, https://dx.doi.org/10.1787/f77157e4-en. [2]

OECD (2019), *Digital Government in Chile – Digital Identity*, OECD Digital Government Studies, OECD Publishing, Paris, https://dx.doi.org/10.1787/9ecba35e-en. [3]

OECD (2019), *The Path to Becoming a Data-Driven Public Sector*, OECD Digital Government Studies, OECD Publishing, Paris, https://dx.doi.org/10.1787/059814a7-en. [7]

OECD (2016), *Digital Government in Chile: Strengthening the Institutional and Governance Framework*, OECD Digital Government Studies, OECD Publishing, Paris, https://dx.doi.org/10.1787/9789264258013-en. [1]

1 Introduction

This opening chapter provides the context for why service design and delivery, specifically in the context of ChileAtiende, is a priority for the government of Chile. To provide context to the overall report the chapter presents a brief history of government services exploring how the nature of their design and delivery has shifted from analogue origins, through the e-government era and is now understood from the perspective of digital government.

“Most of government is mostly service design most of the time” (Edgar, 2015[1]). This statement by the Head of Design for the United Kingdom’s National Health Service reflects the observation that interactions that fall under the responsibility of government do not simply happen by accident but are the product of decisions that influence the design and experience of how government is consumed.

Service delivery is the central point of contact between a state and its citizens, residents, businesses and visitors. It has a major impact on the efficiency achieved by public agencies, the satisfaction of citizens with their government and the success of a policy in meeting its objectives. Alongside confidence in the integrity of government, the reliability and quality of government services is an important contributor to trust in government. The quality of these interactions between citizen and state shape not only their experience of government, but influence the opportunities they access and the lives they build. The digital transformation of our economies and societies is leading to external pressures for government to improve the delivery of services whilst at the same time motivating the public sector to champion design approaches to better meet the needs of citizens.

In this context, users are unforgiving of services that compare poorly with experiences of high quality delivery, whether from the private sector or elsewhere in government. To meet rising quality expectations, governments need to focus on understanding the entirety of a user’s journey across multiple channels, as well as associated internal, civil servant, processes, to identify opportunities for transforming the end to end experience. Doing this may require adjusting and re-designing processes, defining common standards and building shared infrastructure to create the necessary foundations for transformation as well as ensuring the interoperability of public agencies to facilitate the data flows that will make integrated, omni-channel services possible.

This report, *Digital Government in Chile – improving public service design and delivery*, is intended to meet the needs of the Chilean public sector in understanding the role services play as the point of contact between a State and its citizens and therefore leverage the opportunities provided by the digital age to improve public service design and delivery. The OECD Digital Government and Open Government Data unit has long-standing interest in this area with *Rethinking e-Government Services* (OECD, 2009[2]) arguing for the shift from government-centric to user-centric approaches and *M-Government* (OECD/ITU, 2011[3]) highlighting the importance of meeting the needs of users as conveniently as possible. Informed by the experience of OECD member countries, previous projects and research of the Inter-American Development Bank and OECD Digital Government Reviews carried out around the world (specifically in Estonia and Finland (OECD, 2015[4]), Norway (OECD, 2017[5]), Brazil (OECD, 2018[6]), African Portuguese-Speaking Countries and Timor-Leste (OECD, 2018[7]), Panama (OECD, 2019[8]) and Slovenia (OECD, Forthcoming[9])), the report presents a strategic approach that can be applied to increase the efficiency of public agencies, the satisfaction of citizens with their government, and the success of a policy in meeting its objectives.

A brief history of services

Analogue government

The delivery of services by organisations responsible for health, welfare, safety, security and other areas is a timeless characteristic of countries. It is not just in the twenty first century that governing authorities have wanted to conduct censuses to understand their populations, implemented tax regimes to generate income, recognised the owner of a piece of land or with responsibility for a business, required paperwork to cross from one side of a border to another, or recorded the outcome of a criminal prosecution. It is hard to conceive of a world without the bureaucracy with which we are familiar, and hard to pinpoint a period of history with an absence of these kinds of interaction between citizens and their governing authority.

For the majority of human bureaucratic history those processes and interactions have been carried out with paper and handled manually. Ledgers, dockets, stamps and warehouses filled with boxes and boxes of paper are the more familiar currency of government services than the ideal of proactive and data-driven services with users at their heart which this report will discuss. It is in the origins of government organisation and service logistics that many of the structures and interactions with which we're familiar came into existence, shaped by the practical realities of paper based, siloed activity where a new technology or new policy might give birth to a bespoke organisation, established to respond to a particular, discrete need.

Analogue government therefore has a successful history of dealing with the business of government. To contemporary eyes the history of bureaucracy may look inefficient but paper has underpinned mostly effective government for an awfully long time. Nevertheless, the legacy of these approaches is found in the organising structure of government institutions and the specific design of particular processes in law but also in the networks of service provision criss-crossing a country whether in the interplay between central and local government or in the offices to which people go in order to get their needs met.

That is not to say that paper based service delivery has stood still – those processes have come under scrutiny, been open to innovation and gone through iteration in light of the technological advances of the age all with a view to generate greater efficiency or improved outcomes whether in the public or private sector. Indeed, one of the earliest recorded mentions of a 'one stop shop' can be found in an advert from July 1930 of a car mechanic from Lincoln, Nebraska, USA bringing auto parts, auto repairs and auto sales into a single location[1]. This idea of giving people one destination to resolve their needs rather than travelling to several provided the blueprint for the One Stop Shop concept that has now become synonymous with government efforts to simplify the administrative burden on their citizens and businesses.

E-government

The late twentieth century saw government exploring the opportunities to increase its efficiency and effectiveness through digitising analogue processes. These changes created a driver for exploring further consolidation of services and delivery of e-government. The argument was fairly simple - greater government efficiency would follow not only from reducing the quantity of access points but also the reliance on paper. In general, this model of digitisation considered that technology was the solution for implementing an existing analogue process in terms of encouraging more people to use online services and supporting organisations achieve more with less.

This approach tended to make the implementation of technology the focus, especially in the context of closing down and consolidating any existing physical face-to-face channels. Whilst governments used ICT to streamline the relationship between citizens and business and the public sector there was a desire to make things better. However, sometimes this saw the e-government agenda morph into a 'digital by default' ideal that assessed the cost of continuing to provide services in person as too high and set the expectation for services to be accessible online, and online only with those choosing to continue using offline channels facing higher costs, tighter deadlines and reduced support.

In the rush to make things available online the result has been government-centred services, which is to say, services that reproduce analogue bureaucratic procedures using technology and simply doing the same things that had been done offline, online. This led to results that did not necessarily bring more convenience to the users. Administrative simplification efforts for particular industries and certain audiences as well as a focus on particular life events created consolidated entry points but inadvertently introduced different siloes accompanied by multiple channels (digital, telephone and physical) with different navigation, usability and effectiveness. In reflecting the internal institutional structure of government there is a mismatch with expectations of the twenty-first century in offering simpler and more convenient services that are seamless, integrated and can be accessed across multiple channels.

The enthusiasm for digitising what was previously analogue is best described by the 'digital by default' agenda. Introduced with the best of intentions its application has sometimes risked excluding some parts of society from being able to access critical services. Furthermore, the resulting contractual arrangements with systems integrators, overheads of legacy technologies and siloed approaches to designing policy separate from delivering services separate from ongoing operations have contributed to the environment that has most recently given rise to a digital government agenda.

Digital government

The digital government agenda represents a new paradigm of thinking about the design and delivery of services. Where e-government had a technology focus, digital government is about embedding a digital culture throughout the practice of government that focuses on meeting the need of a user by re-engineering and re-designing services and processes. Technology is a background enabler, woven into the ongoing activity of improving government, rather than the driver of transformation. This digitalisation goes hand in hand with establishing digital-by-design cultures that transform the behaviours of an organisation. The challenge for governments around the world is in building a new relationship between citizen and state and digital government is critical in encouraging an open and user-driven approach that rethinks and redesigns the interactions rather than simply moving bureaucracy from one channel to another.

Figure 1.1. From analogue to digital government

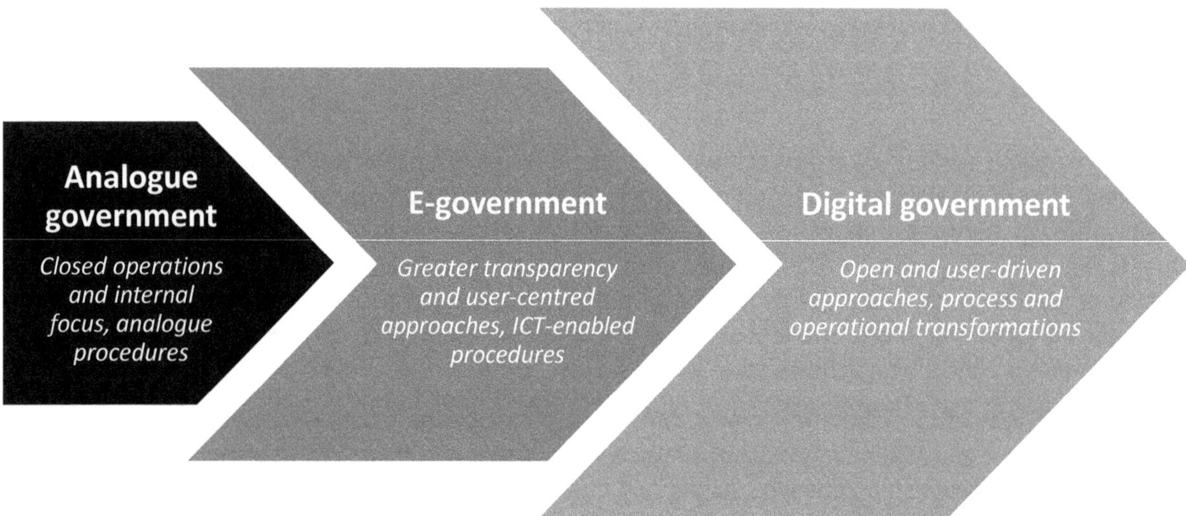

Source: Based on OECD (2014[10]), *Recommendation of the Council on Digital Government Strategies*

The *Recommendation of the Council on Digital Government Strategies* (OECD, 2014[10]) comprises 3 pillars and 12 principles that ensure the successful design, development and implementation of digital government strategies to enable transformation. They reflect a set of activities that, taken together, allow government to address the necessary activities to deliver on the promise of digital transformation. Building on the Recommendation, the OECD has developed a series of indicators to measure the level of country's digital government maturity across six dimensions, as shown in Figure 1.2.

Figure 1.2. The main characteristics of a digital government

Source: OECD (Forthcoming[11]), *Digital Government Policy Framework*

Each of these areas has relevance to supporting the effective implementation of a service design and delivery strategy, which will be discussed in more detail throughout Chapter 2.

1. **Data-driven public sector:** The importance of data as a foundational enabler for designing policies and services, shaping their ongoing delivery and understanding the impact they are having and changes that may need to be made.
1. **Open by default:** The desire of governments to collaborate across organisational boundaries, and involve those outside of government is critical in ensuring that service teams understand and engage with the needs of users and that government itself is able to collaborate and coordinate its activity to solve whole problems.
2. **Government as a platform:** Building an ecosystem of resources and tools that support and equip service design and delivery teams in meeting the needs of their users. This includes sharing best practice and guidelines; governance, spending and assurance; digital inclusion; common components and tools (such as digital identity, notifications, payments and design systems)); data governance and its application for public value and trust; and public sector talent and capabilities.
3. **Digital by design:** Recognising that transforming services needs to be approached with an understanding of all the associated activities rather than simply putting analogue processes online and expecting to improve outcomes.
4. **User-driven:** An approach to designing and delivering services, enabled by an open by default culture and the ambitions of digital by design to include, and be led by, the needs of the public rather than the assumptions of government.
5. **Proactive:** The ability of governments to anticipate, and rapidly respond to, the needs of their citizens through the application of the five above-mentioned dimensions. Transformed government allows problems to be addressed from end to end rather than the otherwise piecemeal digitisation of component parts.

In practical terms digital government provides an opportunity for developing end to end services that understand the interplay in the course of resolving a single issue between analogue interactions (such as an initial letter), face to face interactions, telephone contacts and digital services. As such, the digital government approach to designing and delivering services is not about digital versus analogue but about an approach and methodology that prioritises understanding user needs and designing approaches that meet them.

Despite these ideals, what has often resulted from the evolution of service provision is a jumble of different delivery networks and service channels. Sometimes one stop shops have provided a selection of services grouped around a particular set of needs whilst still maintaining organisational websites that also provide the individual services. In other cases smaller organisations might have collaborated to combine their efforts whilst larger organisations with the resources to operate independently may be running their own offices, websites and call centres. The digital government agenda has begun to see various countries respond to these technical and infrastructure legacies by arguing that if the citizen was at the heart of a particular approach then none of this confusing mess would exist. As such, countries need to outline a strategic plan by which they can transition from the existing status quo to a situation where citizens can access reliably high quality and well-designed services, delivered by teams in government supported by a full range of 'Government as a Platform' resources and capabilities.

Services in Chile

Like many countries, the Government of Chile has taken steps to respond to the patchwork of its services. Motivated by the desire to deliver higher quality services the government of Chile established a centralised, nationwide network of access points under a common branding: ChileAtiende is a multi-channel entry point for government through which citizens can access public services face to face, on the telephone, or through digital means (web, self-service kiosks and social media). Its ambition has been to bring the State closer to citizens through a simpler, more efficient and transparent approach. To date the ChileAtiende network provides services for 25 government institutions, and reaches 71,5% net user satisfaction rate in the standardised measurement (Secretaría de Modernización, 2018[12]) and 89% in the Social Security Institute (*Instituto de Previsión Social*, IPS) independent survey (Instituto de Previsión Social, 2017[13]) in its face-to-face channel, outstanding figures for local satisfaction levels with public services. However, figures for ChileAtiende service delivery are yet modest: the network covers only 6% of total transactions for public service delivery in the country (Ministerio de Hacienda, 2018[14]). Additionally, it only covers a limited number of public institutions in transactional service delivery.

Hence, if ChileAtiende is to become the cornerstone of Chilean public service delivery, it requires more than just an expansion strategy to increase the number of institutions and services provided in person, online and through the call centre, whilst maintaining its current high levels of satisfaction. Scaling ChileAtiende in this way must be complemented by a comprehensive service design and delivery strategy that takes measures to promote a service design culture across the Chilean public sector. This is foundational to Chile achieving high quality user-driven public services across all channels. As maturity of service delivery progresses it will be necessary to explore ways to prioritise the transformation of Chile's more than 3 000 identified services, and to identify any commonalities that can be addressed through a Government as a Platform Strategy.

The Chilean government is ambitious for ChileAtiende to put the state at the service of the citizen, making every effort to avoid friction for people in accessing public goods and services. As they approach the future of service design and delivery in the country, the desire is to serve their citizens not only with agility, efficiency and speed but with care and attention. ChileAtiende is seen as the vehicle through which that can be done because it is a trusted and respected presence in the community providing face to face access to services, facilitated by a design and delivery approach that provides ubiquity and simplicity of access

In the next chapter, this report will present a Conceptual Framework for considering how a country might approach the strategic transformation of the design and delivery of its services leveraging the opportunities provided by the digital age. Chapter 3 will describe the service delivery situation in Chile before Chapter 4 will provide an analysis of that situation against the conceptual framework.

References

Edgar, M. (2015), *Most of government is mostly service design most of the time. Discuss. – Matt Edgar writes here*, https://blog.mattedgar.com/2015/05/12/most-of-government-is-mostly-service-design-most-of-the-time-discuss/ (accessed on 24 January 2019). [1]

Instituto de Previsión Social (2017), *Estudio Recurrente de Satisfacción de Usuarios del IPS.* [13]

Ministerio de Hacienda (2018), *Presentación Nueva Institucionalidad ChileAtiende.* [14]

OECD (2019), *Digital Government Review of Panama: Enhancing the Digital Transformation of the Public Sector*, OECD Digital Government Studies, OECD Publishing, Paris, https://dx.doi.org/10.1787/615a4180-en. [8]

OECD (2018), *Digital Government Review of Brazil: Towards the Digital Transformation of the Public Sector*, OECD Digital Government Studies, OECD Publishing, Paris, https://dx.doi.org/10.1787/9789264307636-en. [6]

OECD (2018), *Promoting the Digital Transformation of African Portuguese-Speaking Countries and Timor-Leste*, OECD Digital Government Studies, OECD Publishing, Paris, https://dx.doi.org/10.1787/9789264307131-en. [7]

OECD (2017), *Digital Government Review of Norway: Boosting the Digital Transformation of the Public Sector*, OECD Digital Government Studies, OECD Publishing, Paris, https://dx.doi.org/10.1787/9789264279742-en. [5]

OECD (2015), *OECD Public Governance Reviews: Estonia and Finland: Fostering Strategic Capacity across Governments and Digital Services across Borders*, OECD Public Governance Reviews, OECD Publishing, Paris, https://dx.doi.org/10.1787/9789264229334-en. [4]

OECD (2014), *Recommendation of the Council on Digital Government Strategies, OECD/LEGAL/0406*, OECD, Paris, https://legalinstruments.oecd.org/en/instruments/OECD-LEGAL-0406. [10]

OECD (2009), *Rethinking e-Government Services: User-Centred Approaches*, OECD e-Government Studies, OECD Publishing, Paris, https://dx.doi.org/10.1787/9789264059412-en. [2]

OECD (Forthcoming), *Digital Government Review of Slovenia*, OECD Publishing, Paris. [9]

OECD (Forthcoming), *OECD Digital Government Policy Framework*, OECD, Paris. [11]

OECD/ITU (2011), *M-Government: Mobile Technologies for Responsive Governments and Connected Societies*, OECD Publishing, Paris, https://dx.doi.org/10.1787/9789264118706-en. [3]

Secretaría de Modernización (2018), *Encuesta de Satisfacción Usuaria.* [12]

Note

[1] The earliest source identified by https://www.phrases.org.uk/meanings/one-stop-shop.html is for an advert for the John Bracelen Company from *The Lincoln Star*, Lincoln Nebraska USA from July 1930.

2 The conceptual framework

This chapter introduces the OECD conceptual framework for service design and delivery using different experiences from OECD member and non-member countries.

First, the context for design and delivery of services looks at politics, legacy channels and technology and the society and geography of a country.

Second, the philosophy for the design and delivery of services considers the leadership and vision provided, and then associated behaviours to embed these ideas within the public sector including understanding, and responding to whole problems; services that make sense from end to end; involving the public; combining policy, delivery and operations across organisational boundaries; and taking an agile approach.

Finally, the different enabling resources to facilitate the design and delivery of services. This includes sharing best practice and guidelines; governance, spending and assurance; digital inclusion; common components and tools; data governance and its application for public value and trust; and public sector talent and capabilities.

Given the context discussed in Chapter 1, there is a need to review how countries might build on previous efforts for administrative simplification or a focus on particular life events to use digital government approaches to meet the needs of citizens through designing proactive, data-driven and omni-channel services with the agility to deploy and effectively embrace emerging technologies where appropriate. To take into account and rationalise the historic context, better embed a service design culture, and mature the conversation about enabling resources the OECD proposes the conceptual framework at Figure 2.1. This provides the basis for analysing the situation facing any country in terms of thinking through its strategic approach to the needs of those interacting and engaging with the state. In presenting the framework this chapter explores different experiences from OECD member countries.

Figure 2.1. A conceptual framework for analysing the design and delivery of services

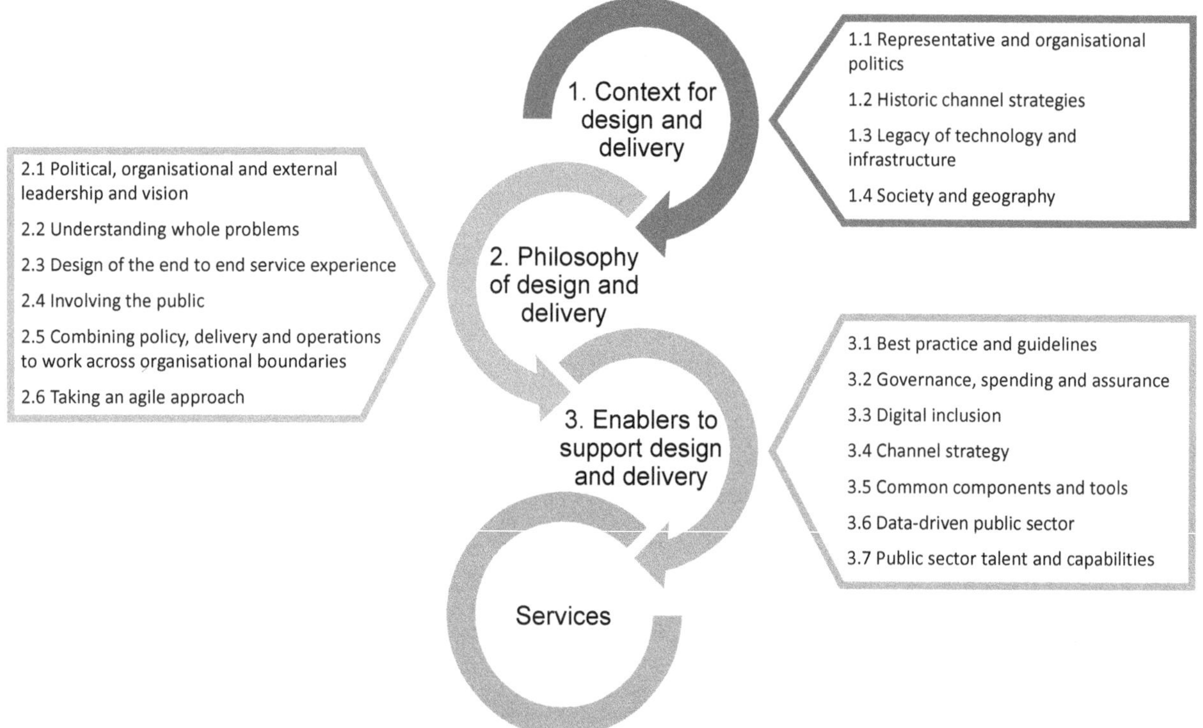

The framework consists of three elements that combine to deliver high quality and reliable services:

1. The context for design and delivery of services: the way in which services are designed and delivered is informed by the history of delivering services (channel strategy) in a country, political support for the agenda, and the role of legacy technology amongst other factors.
2. The philosophy for the design and delivery of services: the activities and practices that direct current activity and contribute to the decisions about the design and delivery of services. This focuses on leadership and vision as well as approaches to service design and delivery itself.
3. The enablers to support the design and delivery of services: the resources that have been developed by countries in order to facilitate teams in the design and delivery of services. This includes sharing best practice and guidelines (including guiding principles, style guides and reference manuals); governance, spending and assurance (including business cases, budget thresholds, procurement, service standards and assurance processes); digital inclusion (including digital literacy, connectivity and accessibility); common components and tools (such as digital identity, notifications, payments and design systems); data governance and its application for public value and trust; and public sector talent and capabilities (including recruitment, communities of practice, training and consultancy).

Context for design and delivery of services

Service delivery is integral to the activity of the public sector and foundational to the experience citizens and businesses have of government. As such, any analysis of the design and delivery of services needs to consider the existing circumstances. In this way, the conversation about service design and delivery reflects the 'contextual factors' identified by the OECD as shaping the governance of digital government. Produced by the OECD Working Party of Senior Digital Government Officials Task Force on Governance, Box 2.1 summarises a framework with which to analyse the context surrounding the entire digital government agenda. Although many, if not all, of them influence the way in which services can be delivered in a country there are some which are important in considering the breadth of channels available to the public and strategically understanding how they can work together.

Box 2.1. Draft contextual factors influencing the governance of digital government

During 2018-2019 the Working Party of Senior Digital Government Officials convened a Task Force to consider the question of the governance for digital government. Their discussions provided the basis for a handbook designed to equip governments with the necessary insights to consider how to approach the overall governance of digital government. The draft proposes framing those discussions around Contextual factors, Institutional models and the Policy levers required to support implementation.

The discussion around contextual factors identified the following themes:

1. **Overall political and administrative culture** including power structure; geopolitical situation; defence and security; legalistic versus non-legalistic system; role of elected governments; nature of regulations; political continuity; extent of autonomy in terms of regional government; the extent to which a country is centralised or decentralised; and procurement culture.
2. **Socio-economic factors** including overall economic climate; digital literacy of the population; levels of e-commerce and adoption of digital within businesses; levels of competitiveness and innovation; public sector digital skills; public trust; societal diversity; migration flows in society.
3. **Technological context** including digital connectivity infrastructure; extent to which government or the private sector has legacy technology; integration of IT and digital into business; government specific technological innovations
4. **Environmental and geographical considerations** including local economies; regional variance and geological risks and hazards

Following the 2019 meeting of the Working Party of Senior Digital Government Officials in Brussels, the Task Force and OECD will continue to develop these ideas and produce materials assisting governments to share and learn from the experiences of responding to the challenges they identify.

Note: Taken from the Draft E-Leaders Governance Handbook prepared for the 2019 meeting of the Working Party of Senior Digital Government Officials and based on discussion amongst the E-Leaders Task Force on Governance (unpublished)

Representative and organisational politics

The *Recommendation of the Council on Digital Government Strategies* (OECD, 2014[1]) identifies the need to encourage engagement and participation of public, private and civil society stakeholders in policy making and public service design and delivery. That is complemented by The *Recommendation of the Council on Open Government* (OECD, 2017[2]) which calls on governments to move towards a "culture of governance that promotes the principles of transparency, integrity, accountability and stakeholder participation in support of democracy and inclusive growth".

The openness with which a government approaches the participation of those outside of government shapes the experience of services, the nature of channels provided and the ongoing design and delivery of government interventions. Although the design and delivery of services is carried out by public servants acting in an apolitical fashion, there is an unavoidable political element to this discussion. The policies that sit behind government services are shaped by the ideologies and commitments of those who have won elections and therefore hold a democratic mandate from the public.

Such dynamics have the potential to politicise the service design and delivery agenda. The emphasis of one service delivery channel or design approach during a particular government or minister's term runs the risk of being reversed or side-lined by their successors. Efforts to depoliticise the agenda and view it as neutral should be encouraged with all sides being able to support efforts to achieve greater financial efficiency and increases in the quality of the citizen experience.

Nevertheless, with digitally enabled omni-channel service design and delivery reconfiguring how people access government, there can be implications for the public sector workforce and particular communities. The financial and user experience cases for consolidating existing channels and simplifying the landscape of service provision may well be compelling but such an analysis might show face-to-face services as most costly and thereby encourage the use of online or telephone based provision and consolidation of offline networks to reduce demand on physical locations. This will successfully reduce staff overheads but it will also narrow options for accessing physical locations. These decisions, ostensibly driven by the politically neutral ambitions of digital government or administrative simplification, are inherently political because they impact on the lives of voters, public servants and communities. As such, 'channel shift' efforts can prompt criticism from politicians, local communities and trades unions. The effect of that criticism can stifle the progress for which there is an ambition and constrain how radical a shift in service provision towards an omni-channel approach is possible.

A final area relates to the organisational structure of service provision in a country. Countries with a high level of centralisation face a different context to those countries with significant local and regional autonomy. However, those nuances may not be clear to the citizen or business trying to access services from 'government'. Achieving high quality services across channels means responding to the particular contextual implications of the interplay between areas under the responsibility of central government, arms-length agencies or local and municipal government. This is particularly relevant in identifying the needs and challenges faced by smaller organisations operating with more limited resources and highlight the opportunities for collaboration or the provision of additional support (as discussed later in this chapter) to achieve a transformed approach to service design and delivery. The United Kingdom's Local Digital Declaration, discussed in Box 2.2 presents one example of how central government and local administrations are responding to this challenge but this is not the only model. In Spain, for example, the national legal framework provides regional and local governments with great autonomy and independence while ensuring they are legally recognised as essential participants in the overall governance for digital transformation. Through a comprehensive and complex governance structure the integration of all key actors is secured the development of enabling solutions such as digital identity, managing company powers, interoperability and document exchange systems.

Box 2.2. The UK's Local Digital Declaration

The UK Local Government sector is geographically and politically diverse with a wide spectrum of understanding around what digital transformation means to an organisation. To support and unite local authorities around a shared understanding of good digital practice the UK's Government Digital Service and Ministry of Housing, Communities and Local Government launched the Local Digital Declaration.

Designed to help local authorities 'fix the plumbing' of digital The Local Digital Declaration forms the basis for local authorities to adopt guiding principles on what good looks like so that regardless of size, location or political governance, any organisation can follow them. It is because so many local authorities have tried and failed to digitally transform in isolation that there is such groundswell and support for a unified approach.

The Declaration addresses the legacy IT contracts, isolation of procurement practices and siloed digital projects that have left local government services vulnerable to high delivery costs and low customer satisfaction for the public they serve. It challenges local and central government, their influencers and the private sector that supplies them, to support "building the digital foundations for the next generation of local public services." It sets out principles that support local authorities to follow open standards and best digital practices with view to developing a common, open approach to digital service transformation across government.

Each signatory of the declaration commits to the co-published principles of good digital and to supporting local authorities in following them. It has been written for local authority leadership to embrace and use as a central point for cultural change that supports the embedding of digital transformation within the organisations.

This is the first collective agreement that has brought central and local government together in consensus on what good digital practice is. It was developed through one-to-one engagement and relationship building. Workshops teased out an understanding of what prevented digital innovation, why procurement was isolated and why change had not been forthcoming. To begin with the Local Digital Declaration had 45 co-publishers and today has over 200 signatories, showing the demand for support and change but also offering testimony to the detailed and exemplary engagement bringing together voices from across the public sector, their influencers and suppliers.

Source: Local Digital and the Ministry of Housing, Communities and Local Government (2018[3]) *The Local Digital Declaration*; OECD Observatory of Public Sector Innovation (2018[4]) *The Local Digital Declaration*

Historic channel strategy

The evolution from analogue to digital government has left a large footprint. The processes, data flows and channels for delivering services that exist are more often than not the product of various central government or institutional channel strategies and other pressures such as those exerted by administrative simplification campaigns.

Some countries (Box 2.3) have recent histories that make it possible to consider the design and delivery of services from the ground up and ensure coordination from the outset. However, the experience for the majority is to find a patchwork of different channels with different responsibilities. While some organisations may have been able to preserve physical locations for providing face-to-face services in other contexts financial pressures and an efficiency agenda will have seen them close. Alongside those channels, the development of different digital and telephone based channels may have taken place without coordination between organisations meaning that users have to visit multiple locations to address a particular need.

Whilst a country, or its organisations, may have a multi-channel approach the lack of synergy between web, telephone and in-person services may mean an interaction begun online cannot be completed in person and vice versa. Furthermore, contractual arrangements relating to call centres may not be compatible with the needs of physical locations or with whoever is providing the online channels. As a result, an omni-channel strategy, that is where all channels are interchangeable in terms of what they provide and the extent to which an issue can be resolved, are more challenging to implement.

Without a unifying strategy for the design and delivery of services the user experience is left confused while the scale of the challenge to rationalise and consolidate may seem insurmountable. Mapping and understanding the landscape of how different channels operate and where opportunities for partnership might be possible is critical to delivering a transformation in the quality of services which citizens and businesses can access.

Box 2.3. Estonia – a no-legacy digital experience

Following independence from the Soviet Union in 1990, Estonia had the opportunity to approach the organisation and development of its public sector with few preconceptions to constrain its decision making and all of the benefits of an emerging digital sophistication. This digital mindset benefitted from a no-legacy culture that allowed the country to develop administrative processes and an organisational culture that exploited digital technologies to deliver services.

As such, not only is the expectation of high quality digital services embedded within the population of the country, it has created a political environment in which digital leadership is highly regarded and innovation encouraged.

Indeed, that experience has translated into the planning efforts of the Estonian government in following the idea of "no legacy" as a principle requiring the redesign of any government information system older than 13 years. It aims to sustain government agility in the longer term by continuously adapting to changes in context. The length was determined based on the length of typical information system life cycles in the private sector and allowing for a "public sector" margin.

Source: Taken from the Draft E-Leaders Governance Handbook prepared for the 2019 meeting of the Working Party of Senior Digital Government Officials and based on discussion amongst the E-Leaders Task Force on Governance (unpublished); OECD (2015[5]) *Public Governance Reviews: Estonia and Finland*

Legacy of technology and infrastructure

A third area that shapes the context for designing and delivering government services are the tangible artefacts that result from previous efforts in this area. Some of those artefacts relate to the infrastructure associated with physical locations: not only in the buildings but in the associated habits formed by citizens and communities around their use. Where this model has been adopted by several networks there can be a duplication of physical locations in the same community. In these cases, there may be efforts to consolidate all services under one roof in order to achieve twin outcomes of simplifying the experience of government and rationalising its property estate.

In realising the strategic opportunities associated with broadening service delivery that and designing responses to the needs of the public face to face service channels remain a critical bridge between the government and citizens. As such, making sense of this physical infrastructure and identifying the potential for all networks to work together in supporting access to services is critical.

Alongside the physical infrastructure there can also be a legacy of brand recognition and awareness. Whilst some parts of society may deal with government on a regular basis there will be those who perhaps interact once a year. For those who seldom deal with government the importance of brand continuity may mean that they are suspicious about any new design if the change is not well communicated. Equally, if websites are to be consolidated and services delivered through new online channels it is critical to maintain the integrity of the internet and 'leave no link behind' so that bookmarks can be maintained (Box 2.4).

Whilst the physical and conceptual traces of previous networks will feature in the public consciousness of service delivery in a country the internal arrangements and technological logistics within government introduce a further layer of complexity. Institutions will have agreements and ways of working that support the delivery of services that cross organisational boundaries, perhaps through accessing data or developing bespoke technical solutions. In some cases these experiences may have been negative, or constraining. Ensuring that valuable relationships can continue while also revisiting those which have proven problematic is an integral factor in achieving greater interoperability and avoiding unintended consequences for the services that have accreted over time.

Indeed, the contractual arrangements between a government institution and the management of its web, telephone or physical service delivery channels is potentially one of the most significant barriers to transformation of the citizen experience. The legacy of existing arrangements may mean that contracts do not have break clauses or would incur significant costs around making the necessary architectural and infrastructure changes to align with a new strategic direction. Nevertheless, this can be helpful as the dates associated with contracts that reflect this sort of situation can shape a country's roadmap and timeline towards its transformation allowing for a more effective and considered prioritisation process to take place.

Box 2.4. #NoLinkLeftBehind, maintaining 1m+ URLs after launching GOV.UK

Over time government web estates expand. Every organisation, each service, and even short lived campaigns might end up with their own domain. As sites decay and are closed down, little thought is given to the URLs stored in bookmarks, on printed materials or buried in other services. Many organisations decide that redirecting sites is an onerous task, so they either redirect all the old links to the front page of the new site, or simply switch the site off in its entirety. When URLs change, the 'strands' of the World Wide Web break and people cannot find what they are looking for.

For the United Kingdom the centrepiece of its digital government agenda is rationalising all citizen facing government websites into a single domain – GOV.UK. This meant over 1 500 domains, containing over 1 million URLs would need to be closed down with the content either being archived, or transitioned onto GOV.UK. Rather than removing those URLs, the team committed creating individual redirections for each and every page so that users either found the archived content or the equivalent page on GOV.UK. Committing to preserve URLs like this isn't just about being good citizens of The Web but about putting users first to ensure that when people follow links and bookmarked pages they do not see '404, Page Not Found'.

Source: Government Digital Service (2012[6]) *No link left behind* (https://gds.blog.gov.uk/2012/10/11/no-link-left-behind/)

Society and geography

The final area to consider in terms of the context for understanding the appropriate blend between online, telephone and face to face based service provision in pursuit of transforming design and delivery of services is the character of the country's population and its geography.

As countries have pursued ever greater levels of digital service provision and sought 'digital by default' approaches to identity or accessing other services a foundational enabler, and constraint, is the level of connectivity experienced in a country. This can either be through the provision of high speed internet to people's homes, the extent to which there is coverage for mobile data connectivity and the affordability of those data connections themselves. Governments may take steps to enshrine access to the internet as seen in **Mexico** where access to the internet has been established as a fundamental right within the constitution with *Mexico Conectado* then supplying internet access to 250,000 public spaces including hospitals, libraries, schools and government offices (Box 2.5). Understanding the connectivity landscape and ecosystem in a country allows for a more sophisticated response to encouraging adoption of services while ensuring the discussion around face to face provision and community internet access is strategic and led by data.

A further factor that can be supported at a community level is around digital inclusion and digital literacy. Supporting citizens to increase their use of digital services and transition away from face to face locations implies that sufficient attention is also given to the needs of those who cannot use online services. In this case physical and telephone locations not only retain an important role in resolving the need of the citizen but in providing training and support to users that give them confidence to try a digital route in future. Nevertheless, some of these challenges are broader than digital literacy and touch on education in general: data from 2016 show that for OECD countries, an average of 54% of individuals with higher education submitted forms through public websites compared to 17% of individuals with lower levels of education (OECD, 2017[7]). Box 2.5 highlights through the 710 000 tablets delivered to schools across **Mexico** to support literacy and digital literacy that the enshrining of internet access as a right is not just about connectivity but about being able to consume it.

Aside from education, there is also evidence to show that level of income and age are further determinants of confidence in using digital services, and consequently likely to influence the extent to which face to face or telephone services are preferred. Data from 2016 show that for OECD countries, about 49% of the richest quartile of society access online services compared to 25% of the poorest and furthermore, while 42% of those aged between 25-54 went online to interact with government, only 24% of people aged 55-74 did so (OECD, 2017[7]). Consequently, a detailed understanding of age, education and income is essential to developing a national strategic approach to the design and delivery of services.

A final area to consider is that of geography. The terrain of a country may impede the ability to deliver full connectivity whilst disparate populations spread out across a wide area will mean face to face provision will never provide full coverage. In Chile, the ChileAtiende network has developed a response to this particular challenge with one in five of its locations not having a permanent office, but instead being served periodically by a mobile venue. This ensures that more remote communities are not denied the opportunities to resolve their issues with the state. In this way a digital channel strategy needs to be aligned with questions of digital inclusion and digital connectivity to ensure that nobody is left behind in the fundamental responsibility of the state to deliver services to citizens. This is well demonstrated by the experience of **Portugal** where the face to face approach offered through its Citizens Shops and Citizen Spots (see Box 2.18) was a necessary complement to its telephone and web-based offering due to the limited levels of internet access within the population at the time.

Box 2.5. Mexico's multi-faceted and coherent approach to digital transformation

In April 2013 Mexico established a governance model for coordinating various activities under its Digital Strategy and later that year, on 11 June 2013 The Telecommunications Amendment was published which provided the legal basis for a complete transformation of the way in which the country approaches its digital transformation.

Central to this transformation is the recognition of access to the internet as a fundamental right, established in the Mexican constitution. Through Mexico Conectado internet access is being brought to 250,000 public spaces including hospitals, libraries, schools and government offices.

However, the approach to digital government in Mexico has a broader focus than internet connectivity:

- The single government website, gob.mx, was launched in August 2015 to be a single point of access for all citizens. It provides access to more than 4000 government services and consolidates 5000 federal government websites.
- A platform where citizens can provide ideas, report corruption and participate in building better services and policies.
- A new ICT policy for improving the way that federal government acquires technology to maximise public value and access better technology. This included launching 'Fixed-Price Contracts' for software licensing and ICT related hiring.
- An Action Plan for implementing the principles of Open Government with a publicly accessible dashboard detailing progress against the commitments at http://tablero.gobabiertomx.org/
- The creation of datos.gob.mx for publishing datasets and the Mexico Open Network as a supporting network of practitioners discussing and sharing experiences with open data
- The launch of "Innovation Agents" to identify and respond to public problems with digital and technology solutions.
- The launch of "Public Challenges" as a means by which citizens could identify and respond to public problems with digital and technology solutions
- A Digital Inclusion and Literacy Program delivered 710 000 tablets for the school year 2014-2015 in 6 states within the Mexican territory

Source: OECD (n.d.[8]) *Digital Government Toolkit – Mexico: National Digital Strategy (https://www.oecd.org/gov/mexico-digital-strategy.pdf)*

Philosophy for the design and delivery of services

Having understood the existing context for the service agenda in a country the next area of focus are the practices that shape and direct the strategic activity associated with the design and delivery of services. This relates to the leadership for the agenda, the vision that it sets and then the way in which service design and delivery is approached.

Leadership and vision

The *Recommendation of the Council on Digital Government Strategies* (OECD, 2014[1]) identifies in its 5th, 6th and 7th provisions the importance of securing the necessary leadership and political commitment to digital government strategies for them to be successful (OECD, 2014[1]). It indicates the need for this to take place through efforts to promote coordination and collaboration, providing clarity about priorities as well as to increase stakeholder engagement and ensuring that the digital government agenda complements and supports other activity within government. Finally it suggests the need for effective organisational and governance frameworks for co-ordinating implementation.

Whilst focused on providing a holistic framework within which to achieve the digital transformation of government as a whole, these ideas are relevant in considering the specifics of service design and delivery. Nowhere is this clearer than at the highest level for elected representatives, their appointees and the senior government officials who lead institutions to recognise the value of putting the application of digital, data and technology at the heart of their country's future. Individuals throughout the public sector can provide localised leadership and inspire their colleagues to deliver value. However, there is no substitute for the momentum that follows from a clear vision that is owned and shared throughout government for understanding the needs of citizens and including them in the design of their resolution.

Political leadership

From the perspective of political leadership this includes having a clearly expressed vision for the role of digital in the future of the country and as an extension, the implications for service design and delivery. The experience of **Estonia** (Box 2.3) recognised the value of having a commonly understood role for digital amongst a country's political leadership from an early stage. In **Panama**, during the 2019 Presidential election, each candidate made it clear that digital, data and technology were a priority (OECD, 2019[9]).

Having such leadership from the top helps to show that the application of digital, data and technology is not optional but sits at the heart of what a country will be trying to do. As a result, it makes it easier to establish an agenda supported by appointed minsters and that will consequently spread throughout government because there is a mandate from the very top (as seen in **Norway** Box 2.6). In Chile, several important aspects of the digital government agenda have been enshrined in the Digital Transformation of the State Law (MINSEGPRES, 2019[10]).

As discussed earlier in this chapter (Representative and organisational politics) there can be challenges in having too visible a political champion but this needs to be set against the importance of having the political capital and influence to be able to effect the necessary changes in support of rethinking and redesigning services. Without a clear mandate to address the patchwork of different channels and organisational fiefdoms arriving at a consensus may prove difficult. It is not always sufficient for government leaders to provide funding and other incentives to change the status quo.

Box 2.6. The Norwegian "Digital First Choice" initiative

The Digitalisation Memorandum (Digitaliseringsrundskrivet) in Norway established that the government should communicate with citizens and businesses through digital services that are comprehensive, user-friendly, safe, and designed to ensure everyone can access them.

In order to achieve this the Memorandum set out specific delivery criteria:

- By the end of 2017, ministries were required to map the potential for digitalising services and processes with supporting plans for how all appropriate services would then be made available digitally.
- By the end of 2018, ministries would look at their services in relation to those provided by other organisations and consider whether it is possible to develop 'service chains' offering end to end user journeys and solving whole problems. As part of this expectation, plans and strategies for developing those combined services would be developed.

As part of the mapping exercise Norwegian organisations were to identify whether or not services were already digitalised and, if not, assess their level of suitability. The exercise was also designed to assess the quality of existing services in terms of the extent to which they were user-driven, user-centred and user-friendly and judge whether they needed to be re-designed, simplified or even eliminated.

Furthermore, the Digitalisation Memorandum required not only that services were analysed but that the relevant regulatory framework and legislation be reviewed.

Source: OECD, (2017[11]) *Digital Government Review of Norway: Boosting the Digital Transformation of the Public Sector*

Organisational leadership

While elected representatives set the political direction and high level vision, responsibility for implementing that intent and delivering on the ambitions of government belongs to the civil service. The OECD's previous work concerning the governance of digital government in Chile (OECD, 2016[12]) highlighted the importance of clearly identifying leadership from an institution to coordinate the strategy and priorities for transformation. Given the relevance of the digital government agenda to the transformation of government services in a country there are benefits to this leadership coming from the same organisation, or if that is not possible, ensuring close coordination.

Indeed, it is critical that leadership of the service design and delivery agenda is understood as a coordinating role and works closely with leaders across the public sector to embed the importance of designing and delivering high quality services in the day to day work of the civil service as a whole. This is particularly important in securing the overall commitment to transforming cross-cutting services that involve multiple parts of the public sector to decrease the potential for duplicated effort.

Civil servants collectively need to embrace the importance of digital transformation in respect of service delivery and work together to open up data, and contribute to the discussions about shared, reusable resources. Nevertheless, inadequate institutional coordination among relevant agendas, such as those on the digital transformation, public services and regulatory reform, can impede a shift of approach towards a coherent use of existing and emerging opportunities to deliver improved service experiences to users.

External leadership

Finally, there is an important leadership role provided by those who are neither elected by the public, nor employed by government. Government cannot choose its users or market services to only a subset of the population and so non-government experiences come with certain caveats but an external perspective can help identify priorities for the service design and delivery agenda, highlight areas that might otherwise be missed and consider how to encourage greater adoption in society. The strategic discussion about services in a country, and digital government itself, will benefit from the insight of academia, civil society and the private sector, as well as the experiences of other countries, to ensure a rounded view of the issues.

Behaviours of service design and delivery

With the necessary leadership identified and strategic direction provided it becomes necessary to think about the characteristics of a service design and delivery culture and how associated good practices might be established and nurtured throughout the public sector. For some parts of government, this will mean making the transition from analogue government straight to digital government approaches whilst in others there will already be a track record in providing e-government services perhaps through administrative simplification efforts or a focus on individual life events. Both situations present their own challenges for subsequently framing desired behaviours around service design and delivery.

This section will consider several of the behaviours of service design and delivery whose presence in a country can contribute to better meeting the needs of the public and transforming their experience of interacting with government. It will look at understanding, and responding to, a whole problem; services that make sense of the end to end experience; involving the public in design and delivery; combining policy, delivery and operations to work across organisational boundaries; and taking an agile approach.

Whether government is considering the renewal of a single service or looking to transform the entirety of government services the scalability of service design and delivery is critical. In doing so it is important to start from a clear and effective definition of 'services' and to consequently prioritise those working practices that help deliver against that vision. Box 2.7 presents the work of the Working Party of Senior Digital Government Officials (E-Leaders) Thematic Group on Service Delivery and a summary of principles to underpin the design of good services proposed by Lou Downe, one of the leading voices in government service design.

Box 2.7. Overarching principles for designing, and delivering, services

Proposed General Principles for Digital Service Delivery

Under the auspices of the Working Party of Senior Digital Government Officials (E-Leaders), OECD member countries have been considering what constitutes best practice in this area for several years. At the 2017 meeting in Lisbon, Portugal, the Thematic Group on Digital Service Delivery presented a set of General Principles that both member countries and other governments could follow. These principles emerged from the experiences of member countries in implementing their digital agendas.

1. User driven - Optimize the service around how users can, want, or need to use it, including cultural aspects rather than forcing the users to change their behaviour to accommodate the service.
2. Security and privacy focused - Uphold the principles of user security and privacy to every digital service offered.
3. Open standards - Freely adopted, implemented and extended standards.
4. Agile methods - Build your service using agile, iterative and user-centred methods
5. Government as a platform - Build modular, API enabled data, content, transaction services and business rules for reuse across government and 3rd party service providers
6. Accessibility - Support social inclusion for people with disabilities as well as others, such as older people, people in rural areas, and people in developing countries.
7. Consistent and responsive design - Build the service with responsive design methods using common design patterns within a style guide
8. Participatory process updating - Design a platform to take into account civic participation in the services updates.
9. Performance measurements - Measure performance such as Digital take-up, User satisfaction, Digital Service Completion Rate and Cost per transaction for a better decision-making process.
10. Encourage Use - Promote the use of digital services across a range of channels, including emerging opportunities such as social media.

Source: Proposed General Guidelines for Digital Service Delivery prepared for the 2017 meeting of the Working Party of Senior Digital Government Officials (Unpublished)

15 principles of good service design

Lou Downe was the Head of Design for the United Kingdom government during the expansion of its service design profession into an established part of the digital, data and technology professional framework for civil service. In that role they encountered lots of teams wanting to know what a good service looked like but found that the service design profession had not developed a language for talking about the purpose of designing services. That prompted them to define that a good service must:

1. Enable a user to complete the outcome they set out to do
2. Be easy to find
3. Clearly explain its purpose
4. Set the expectations a user has of it
5. Be agnostic of organisational structures
6. Require the minimum possible steps to complete
7. Be consistent throughout

8. Have no dead ends
9. Be usable by everyone, equally
10. Respond to change quickly
11. Work in a way that is familiar
12. Encourage the right behaviours from users and staff
13. Clearly explain why a decision has been made
14. Make it easy to get human assistance
15. Require no prior knowledge to use

Source: Downne, (2019[13]), *Good Services: How to Design Services that Work*; Downe, (2018[14]), *15 principles of good service design*

Understanding, and responding to, a whole problem

"Public-facing services allow citizens or their representatives to achieve a desired outcome" (Pope, 2019[15]) and as such the act of designing, and then delivering those services is not a theoretical pursuit but a practical exercise in working with the affected people and adding value to their lives. In order to do that, the first characteristic is to understand the problem in order to respond to what is found rather than setting out to implement what has been imagined.

The starting point for services will be either a newly identified policy intent, or an existing approach to a long-standing problem. In both cases, service design approaches will help to understand the opportunities to deliver value against the policy intent and how the service might practically make sense of the existing landscape. In contrast to sectoral or organisation focused administrative simplification developing that understanding will require looking across the whole of government to understand how different activities are contributing to, or detracting from, the desired policy outcome. Responding to what has been found in order to better meet needs may then require a fundamental redesign of the service, or more minor tweaks to the way in which government is working. Service design involves working out how the existing landscape of government provision fits together, analysing the extent to which needs are being met through them and then identifying how to reconfigure or redesign the approach to improve things.

Taking this approach is important because if a service (whether newly developed, or existing) isn't immediately understood then people can get confused, make mistakes, or decide not to use it. When that happens it increases the effort government has to invest in order to resolve any issues, and the burden on the citizen to deal with the issue they had in the first place.

Box 2.8. Redesigning the Disability Certificate in Argentina

In Argentina, an estimated 3 million people have some disability. To certify this disability, the Medical Evaluation Boards (MEB) distributed throughout the country issue a *Certificado Único de Discapacidad* (disability certificate, CUD) that allows people to access the rights and benefits provided by the Government. According to the National Agency for Disability, 1,405,687 certificates have been issued to the present.

However, despite being a right, the process for obtaining a CUD was a painful and difficult process. There was no digital service to support it with the result that the process could last up to seven months as it involved four steps that required the user to go to a public office in person to:

1. Find out what documentation would be required according the disability and age of the person
2. Submit the documentation and make an appointment to be evaluated;
3. Attend the evaluation by the MEB;
4. Receive a paper certificate.

Not only was the turnaround slow but the process itself was adding extra burdens and complexity to people's lives at a point where they needed increased levels of support.

Having identified that this was a service in need of transformation the National Agency for Disability paired with the team at Mi Argentina, Argentina's platform for providing citizen centred services to carry out a rediscovery and transformation of the service. This multi-disciplinary team was made up of not only software engineers and designers but also psychologists, political scientists, anthropologists and sociologists. Together the team set out not only with the intent of simplifying and speeding up the process but in coming alongside people as they carry out a difficult process and providing them with the service they deserve.

To do this the team carried out user research by interviewing people with disabilities, their families and health workers. As they built up a picture of the challenges people faced they identified opportunities for simplifying the process and designing an approach that could be carried out online in one step (as opposed to the previous 4).

A wizard now guides citizens through the requirements of their application rather than requiring them to attend a physical meeting to establish what documentation is required. The physical meeting is still required but an online appointment system schedules the interview, meaning that users can avoid hours of waiting in queues. Finally, the service proactively provides notifications in the citizen's digital profile ensuring the user knows when the CUD is expiring and offering to help with its renewal.

Developing the solution was only part of the challenge because the solution needed to work with the 453 separate MEBs. This is a challenge because of the political structure surrounding MEBs as well as practical considerations like availability of internet access, furthermore the service delivery culture of the MEBs is not guaranteed to be citizen centred. In response the team developed a strategy that would address the relationship between central government and the MEBs, support the practicalities of connectivity and focus on developing the necessary skills through training whilst iterating the CUD service as they learn more about it.

Source: OECD Observatory of Public Sector Innovation, (2018[16]) *Redesign of the Unique Certificate of Disability*

Services that make sense of the end to end experience

Because government services have often evolved over time with different policy initiatives leading to different interactions a user's journey can often be somewhat fragmented and hard to trace across different parts of government and different channels. The most effective citizen experiences should not require a detailed knowledge of the inner workings of government or involve the burden of working out how best to meet a need across a myriad of different websites, call centres and service delivery locations. They should instead lead users through a simple to complete process and where possible reuse data to anticipate and proactively address aspects that might otherwise have involved further interactions.

In addition to successfully achieving the impression of seamless government, regardless of the messy reality 'behind the scenes', a service design approach prioritises handling the transition between physical, offline and digital elements of a service. Ultimately, a service should be understood:

- from when someone first attempts to solve a problem through to its resolution (from end to end)
- on a continuum between citizen experience and back-office process (external to internal)
- across any and all of the channels involved (omni-channel).

One of the unintended consequences of a 'digital by default' agenda was to create situations where difficulties were introduced for those who had a preference, or a need, to access services in person. Following a 'digital by design' approach recognises the value that can be added to face to face channels when services are developed in a channel agnostic way that enables users to access a given service at any point in the end to end process of meeting their need, according to their most convenient channel.

Box 2.9. Transforming the Justice system in Panama from end to end

In 2012, Panama's National Authority for Government Innovation (Autoridad Nacional para la Innovación Gubernamental, AIG) began working with the country's Justice system to rethink the experience of justice across its several branches of government.

The collaboration involved all the necessary stakeholders and saw a transformative approach taken to the end to end experience in delivering the Accusatory Penal System (Sistema Penal Acusatorio, SPA), which provides the foundation to the way in which courts operate.

AIG's designers took the existing, complex process and broke it into its constituent parts in order to arrive at an understanding of the needs of both those accessing the services and those providing them. This made it possible to prioritise particular elements of the journey and address different elements over time. By 2018, this resulted in transforming not only existing digital elements but also the issues related to physical infrastructure and analogue interactions in the entire experience of justice. There is no longer any paper involved and it has reduced the time involved by 96%.

Source: OECD (2019[9]) *Digital Government Review of Panama: Enhancing the Digital Transformation of the Public Sector*

Involving the public in design and delivery

In order to understand the whole problem, teams working on designing and delivering services need to work with the people who need to use the service. Digitally transformed public services need to engage their users as early in the process as possible. This allows the design process to reflect their views, needs and aspirations from the outset. Such an approach is in line with principle 2 of the *Recommendation of the Council on Digital Government Strategies* (OECD, 2014[1]).

The principles of digital government change the way in which services can be designed and implemented. They create opportunities for citizen-driven activity and civic participation in terms of sharing views, collaborating with peers and expressing dissatisfaction. Service teams that stimulate opportunities for citizens to work with them can embrace innovation and rapidly normalise emerging technology where it can add most value. Having a deep understanding of user needs and an openness to citizen involvement in the process of policy design and service delivery, as seen in Box 2.10, mean teams are well positioned to consider all possible opportunities to apply technology and be agile enough to take advantage when new things arrive.

Partnerships can be developed with community groups and other stakeholders to meet the community and ensure that their experiences shape how government services operate. This approach is exemplified by the experiences of **Canada** and **Portugal** in travelling throughout their countries to engage with the community of their users. In **Portugal**, updating the Simplex model of service delivery (discussed in more detail under Channel Strategy) involved a tour of the regions covering 10 000 kms, speaking to 2 000 people and collecting 1 400 contributions focused on improving the lives of Portuguese citizens (Welby, 2019[17]).

Face to face opportunities not only provide tangible evidence of a responsive government seeking to include the voices of their citizens in the design and application of digital government they can introduce new opportunities to enhance the technical skills and confidence of the public in using online channels, as well as increase their awareness. Supporting citizens to use the internet to access government services has broader benefits in empowering and enabling them to take advantage of other online services.

Box 2.10. Designing and implementing a citizen centric employment services system in Australia

In January 2018 the Australian government appointed an independent Expert Advisory Panel to advise on the future of employment services in the country. The panel considered it was fundamental for the design of future employment services to centre on users. With this focus, the panel heard from around 1 400 unique users across a range of different methods from face-to-face consultations, a public discussion paper and user-centred design research.

Users were engaged to prototype and test policy options through design research workshops, focus groups and one-on-one interviews. The process involved 550 users of employment services including job seekers and employers. User research was conducted across six metropolitan and regional locations with panel members attending sessions to engage with users first hand.

Those experiences shaped the publication of the department's discussion paper which was followed by an extensive consultation across Australia in all the capital cities and selected regional centres. The consultation process involved both roundtables and community forums reaching 540 people (Figure 2.2). Alongside the consultation process 451 unique written submissions were received with 328 of those coming from individuals, more than 50% of whom identified as job seekers.

Figure 2.2. Attendees at consultation round-tables

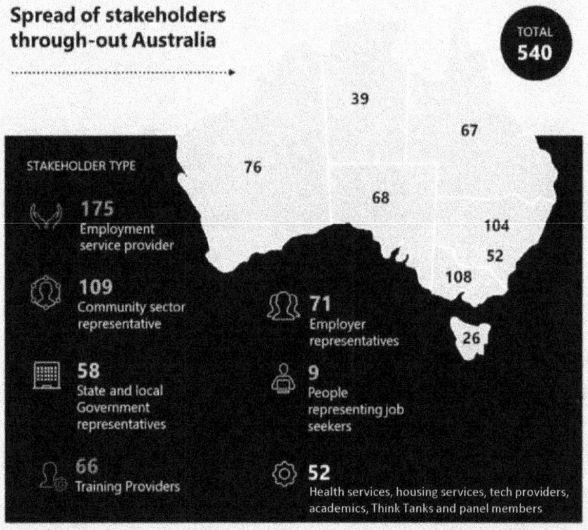

Source: Department of Jobs and Small Business (2018[18]), *Employment Services 2020: Consultation report*

Ultimately, the proposed new employment services model was endorsed and pilots began in March 2019. The service involves a new digital platform that will provide personalised support to all job seekers, with many intended to self-service online. Additional support is available to more disadvantaged job seekers with incentives available to those providing support to them in person.

The new model is being piloted in two regions before being rolled out nationally in 2022. During that period consultation and user-design efforts will continue.

Source: OECD Observatory of Public Sector Innovation (2018[19]), *Design and implementation of a citizen centric employment services system;* Department of Jobs and Small Business (2018[18]), *Employment Services 2020: Consultation report*, Commonwealth of Australia (2018[20]), *I want to work: Employment Services 2020 Report*

Combining policy, delivery and operations to work across organisational boundaries

Successfully transforming service delivery necessitates changes to approaches to both policy making and implementation processes. The status quo has been for policy teams to develop an approach which is then handed over to a commissioning team that instructs an external supplier to deliver against a specification and who, in turn, hand the delivered service over to a fourth team to operate.

When policy decisions are taken in isolation from delivery realities, and operational teams have no ongoing relationship with either, then siloes form. Such a disconnected approach causes problems for both the people accessing the service and government itself. Badly designed services benefit neither political objectives, or meet the needs of the public.

The digital government approach recognises the importance of bringing policy, delivery and operations together throughout the implementation lifecycle to ensure a common vision and coordinated development process. As such, it should be an ambition for those designing and delivering services to unite what might otherwise be siloed as a single team, focused on solving a particular problem together, shown in Figure 2.3.

Figure 2.3. Two paradigms of delivering policy and services

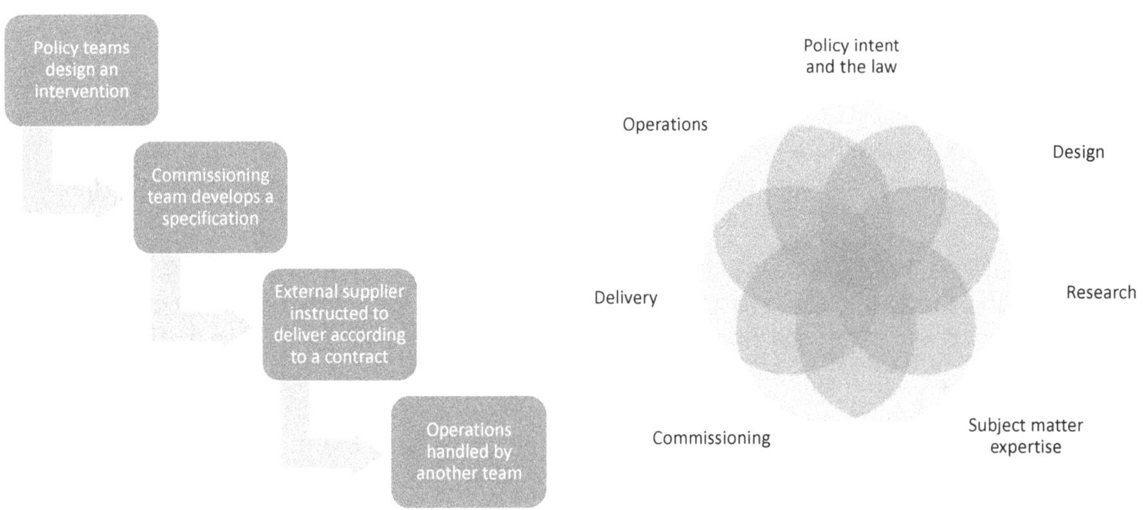

Transformed services rely on diverse, multi-disciplinary teams of designers, developers, subject matter experts, policy officials, lawyers, operational staff, user researchers and content professionals that bring together different perspectives and commit to working across organisational boundaries. Taking a cross-discipline approach and involving those from across government helps to better understand the needs of all users. This idea includes the needs of civil servants within government with the responsibility for administering a service and sits behind the creation of the One Team Government movement (Box 2.11).

Developing cross-government service communities help to create a clear mission that unites all those involved with solving a particular problem for citizens or businesses. In doing so, they help to address several of the other behaviours discussed earlier in the chapter. In the **United Kingdom**, this approach has seen the creation of 4 different communities involving 236 members from 15 organisations with results ranging from simplifying content and user journeys for members of the public through to the redesign of internal procurement processes (Government Digital Service, 2019[21]).

Box 2.11. OneTeamGovernment

In the summer of 2017 a conversation between two civil servants in the United Kingdom planted the seed for the idea of a gathering that wasn't structured around existing tribes of 'policy makers' and 'service designers' but was focused on bringing civil servants together to talk about shared problems and common goals.

Three months later, 186 people gathered together for an event called One Team Government. It was expected that this would be a one-off but after the success of the event meant those who arranged it were inspired to see it become a community of practitioners shaping the conversation in government.

The community has seven principles:

1. Work in the open and positively
2. Take practical action
3. Experiment and iterate
4. Be diverse and inclusive
5. Care deeply about citizens
6. Work across borders (professions, departments, sectors and countries)
7. Embrace technology

Following that first event in London in 2017, these principles have been adopted by chapters in countries and governments around the world. July 2018 saw the first global event with 700 public servants from 43 countries coming together in London in an unconference format to explore how they might share their knowledge and work together to better meet the needs of their users.

In a demonstration that the movement is now truly international and not simply reliant on the original team in London, the 2019 global event took place in Canada where another global gathering discussed 40 different topics with a common theme emerging around improved communication and effective talent management.

Note: A summary of discussions from the 2019 unconference is available here: https://medium.com/oneteamgov/the-2019-oneteamgov-global-report-2fa952dfb37d
Source: Welby (2019[17]), *The impact of Digital Government on citizen well-being*

Taking an agile approach

Both the *Recommendation of the Council on Digital Government Strategies* (OECD, 2014[1]) and the *Recommendation of the Council on Open Government* (OECD, 2017[2]) place a high premium on ensuring that as governments develop policies and services the public should be involved. Nevertheless, there are different ways and extents to which the ideal of user-driven approaches might be approached during the policy making, service delivery and ongoing operational lifecycle.

The public might be engaged by governments through consultation during the policy design process, in seeking the experience of those affected during pilots during the initial implementation phase and gathering feedback once something is operational. However, as shown in Figure 2.4, these are usually independent of one another, do not feed from one into the next and are generally reactive rather than reflecting and mutual ongoing discussion. A result of this is that policy consultation is siloed from the insights derived from both testing a service before it launches and operational feedback once it is live. As a result, the public end up being secondary to the views and activities of public service teams who are not empowered to understand or deliver against outcomes that transform the wellbeing of citizens.

Figure 2.4. A traditional approach to the interaction between government and the public during policy making, service delivery and ongoing operations

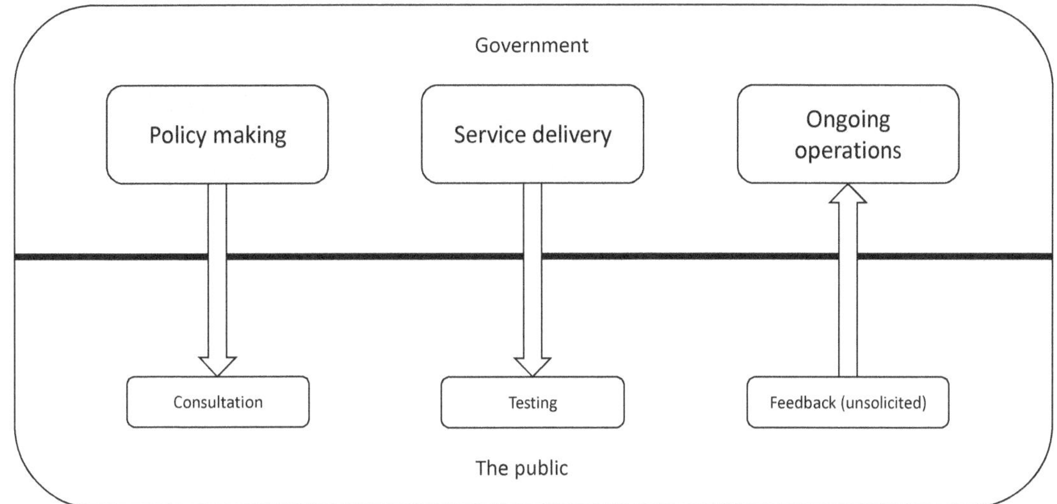

This situation contributes to the siloed delivery approaches discussed in the previous section (Figure 2.3) and as a symptom of Waterfall approaches to delivery. The traditional Waterfall approach is built around a sequencing of activities or phases that must be completed before moving on to the next. This approach attempts to manage uncertainty by creating a plan up front. In this way requirements are identified as a distinct phase before any work is undertaken. There is then no interaction with the solution or any opportunity to provide feedback until the final product is delivered. You only have one chance to get each part of the project right, because you do not return to earlier stages. Should any change want to be made there are high costs associated with what may need to be the revisiting of fundamental decisions.

In contrast, the Working Party of Senior Digital Government Officials (E-Leaders) Thematic Group on Service Delivery advocates for governments to adopt an Agile methodology (Box 2.7). The core values of Agile were first set out in the context of software engineering in the Agile Manifesto below.

> *We are uncovering better ways of developing software by doing it and helping others to do it. Through this work we have come to value:*
>
> *Individuals and interactions over processes and tools*
>
> *Working software over comprehensive documentation*
>
> *Customer collaboration over contract negotiation*
>
> *Responding to change over following a plan*
>
> *That is, while there is value in the items on the right, we value the items on the left more (Beck et al., 2001[22])*

These ideas are increasingly a staple of digital government. Agile involves embracing uncertainty and expecting to continuously learn and improve approaches based on what is learnt in order to prioritise adding value to users as quickly as possible. All the elements found in a Waterfall process are instead carried out concurrently: the activity associated with gathering requirements, planning, designing, building and testing. By starting small with Discovery and Alpha phases teams can research, prototype, test and learn about the needs of their users before committing to building a real service allowing them to fail quickly and correct course in response to what they find. The development of that real service only goes live when enough feedback has been gathered to demonstrate that needs are met and the service works.

Fundamental to this change in approach is the importance of ongoing research and a cyclical model of delivery, Figure 2.5. The separation between the public and government in Figure 2.4 is replaced with government engaging the public on an ongoing basis to explore user-driven approaches and carry out research.

Figure 2.5. An Agile approach to the interaction between government and the public during policy making, service delivery and ongoing operations

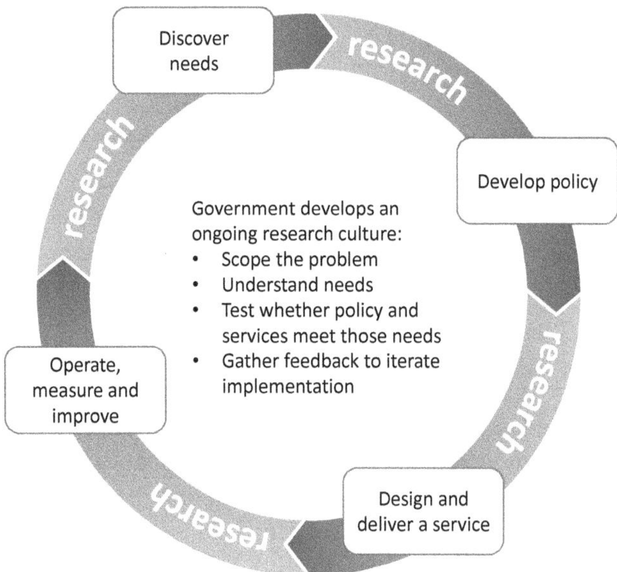

As a result, instead of being initiated in government, policy responds to an understanding of citizen needs based on research conducted with them, reflecting views expressed across a wide sample of the population and informed by insights available from societal data. Having knowledge of the problem in this way allows for the development of policy to be guided and led by the needs of the public rather than the implementation of assumed or paternalistic solutions devised by public servants at their desks. With policy development taking place in close proximity to those carrying out the delivery of the service, research findings can be incorporated into the design and delivery of the service itself. Experimental, hypothesis led interventions involving the public further confirm whether or not a given approach will be effective. At launch, when the policy and any associated services are impacting on real lives, the agile, research-led approach emphasises the continued understanding of the user's experience to establish impact and respond to any insights in understanding whether the policy is having its desired outcomes.

Enablers to support the design and delivery of services

Simply taking into account the contextual factors influencing the way in which services will be designed and delivered, and setting out a vision for doing so may create a situation that feels daunting in terms of putting transformation into action. Countries may have upwards of 3 000 individual services and it will be slow, expensive and inefficient to redesign and rethink each of those from scratch. Therefore, the provision of 'Government as a Platform' enablers are fundamental for helping all those designing and delivering public services to meet the needs of their users at scale, and with pace, while protecting quality and trust.

The OECD considers Government as a Platform to be one of the foundational characteristics of digital government approaches. As a concept there are several ways in which it can be understood whether in supporting service teams, stimulating a marketplace for public services, or rethinking the relationship between citizen and state. These approaches are not mutually exclusive and represent something of a sequential, iterative approach towards creating the conditions for open and innovative government.

Taking the steps to build an ecosystem which supports and equips public servants to make policy and deliver services whilst also encouraging collaboration with citizens, businesses, civil society and others is critical to transforming the process by which services are designed and delivered. The idea of technical shared platforms is not new. The history of e-government contains many examples of shared services and technical interventions designed to offer common solutions to common problems. As a result, enablers can be thought of simply as technology driven interventions. However, this is to overlook the model imagined by Government as a Platform of creating a more holistic ecosystem that provides the resources that can create the conditions in which service design and delivery flourishes and where technology choices are secondary to a focus on the problems facing a particular subset of the public.

It is important to recognise that 'Government' is not a single entity but a collection of organisations and teams who work on designing, implementing and operating policy and the services it produces. Consequently, we start with the practical implications of delivering Government as a Platform with the service teams responsible for meeting the needs of citizens. Those teams may consist entirely of in-house capability, they may be outsourced, they may be a hybrid of the two or they may even be delivered independently of government by charities or private companies. Nevertheless, it is their activity which forms the intermediary between government and users and it is in support of their delivery that an ecosystem focused on common needs can abstract away many of the issues which people would otherwise have to do. This section considers eight areas of enabling practices and activities that fit within this Government as a Platform model and can prove transformative in simplifying and accelerating the design and delivery of services. They are:

- Best practices and guidelines (including style guides and service manuals)
- Governance, spending and assurance (including business cases, budgeting thresholds, procurement and service standards and assurance processes)
- Digital inclusion focused activities (including digital literacy, accessibility and connectivity)
- The channel strategy (emphasising an omni-channel model)
- Common components and tools (including design systems, hosting and infrastructure, digital identity, notifications, payments, and low code)
- Data-driven public sector approaches (including strategic, tactical and operational activities)
- Talent (including recruitment and professions, communities of practice, consultancy and coaching, skills training and skills transfer)

Best practice and guidelines

The first way of enabling teams to deliver high quality services that meet the needs of their users is in providing guidance and materials that can offer insight into the practical steps that can be taken.

Style guide and language

The shift from analogue, via e-government, to digital government has often resulted in a separation of responsibility for serving information to the public and delivering transactions completed by the public. However, to develop services in line with the behaviours discussed earlier in this chapter it is important to recognise the important role that content and language play in the understanding the public might have and therefore the consequent effectiveness of any services that they are consuming.

One way of supporting this is to develop style guides that create consistency and set standards in terms of written communication, whether that is found in letters received through the post, forms completed as part of a transaction, emails triggered by completing a step in process workflow or the web content arrived at from searching the internet. A selection of these are presented in Box 2.12.

Box 2.12. Style guides that support the delivery of services

The Norwegian Clear Language Project (Norway)

The Norwegian Agency for Public Management and eGovernment (*Difi*) collaborates with the Norwegian Language Council to encourage user-friendly language in the delivery of public services:

- *The Golden Pen*: an online course helping editors in the public sector to write in ways that citizens can understand.
- *klarspråk.no*: a website containing practical tools, advice and tips on how to make the language used in service delivery processes clear and user-friendly.
- *Funding Schemes*: agencies can apply for financial support for clear language work. In 2016, two support schemes were made available: one for textual vision and one for measuring the effects of language proficiency.
- *Clear Language Prize*: an annual award given to public agencies that make an extraordinary effort to use clear and user-friendly language in communicating with citizens and businesses.

Source: OECD, (2017[11]), *Digital Government Review of Norway: Boosting the Digital Transformation of the Public Sector*

Style Guides by Government Agencies (United States of America)

In the United States, https://digital.gov catalogues 25 different style guides in use across the public sector and encourages public servants to participate in a plain language community of practice. One of the most notable style guides belongs to 18F. It not only covers questions relating to grammar and spelling but also provides guidance in developing 'user-centred content' built around five principles:

1. Start with user needs.
2. Write in a way that suits the situation.
3. Do the hard work to make it simple.
4. Use plain language and simple sentences. Choose clarity over cleverness.
5. Write for everyone.
6. Respect the complexity of our users' experiences.
7. Build trust.
8. Talk like a person. Tell the truth. Use positive examples and concrete examples
9. Start small and iterate.
10. Make sure your content works for users. Don't be afraid to scrap what's there and start over. Write a draft, test it out, gather feedback, and keep refining

Source: Digital.gov, (n.d.[23]), *Style Guides by Government Agencies* (https://digital.gov/resources/style-guides-by-government-agencies/)

The Government Digital Service Style Guide (United Kingdom)

The Government Digital Service style guide covers style, spelling and grammar conventions for all content published on GOV.UK. It helps to set standards on how to write using "plain English", bringing consistency to the way government talks to its users and making it as inclusive and simple as possible, across all government services.

Source: GOV.UK, (2016[24]), *A to Z – Style Guide – Guidance – GOV.UK* (https://www.gov.uk/guidance/style-guide/a-to-z-of-gov-uk-style)

Service manuals

It is not only in the area of content that the shift to digital government introduces a completely different paradigm in terms of the design and delivery of services as discussed in the previous chapter. Blurring the distinctions between historically separated siloes while also introducing skills around user research and agile delivery mean that several countries have developed resources that act as reference materials to embed and establish a particular design culture.

In addition, the development of strategic approaches to the delivery of common technology (discussed later in this section) has also seen countries develop centralised references for architectural decisions and the documentation of associated APIs and integrations. A selection of these are discussed in Box 2.13.

Box 2.13. Service manuals that support the delivery of services

Arquitectura TI (Colombia)

The Colombian IT Architecture Knowledge Base contains all the materials for ensuring that teams deliver against the provision of the country's Reference Framework for digital government. It includes strategic documents to provide overall understanding, standards identifying technical specifications, step by step guidance materials for engendering a common approach to delivery, shared best practices, the necessary legal underpinnings and a proposed management model to align delivery and strategy within Colombian public sector organisations.

Source: https://mintic.gov.co/arquitecturati/630/w3-propertyvalue-8061.html

GOV.UK Service Manual (United Kingdom)

The United Kingdom's Service Manual is actively maintained by a team of content designers who work with the different professional communities (design, delivery, product, research, etc.) to establish best practice and document it to resource other teams throughout the government, and the wider public sector.

Source: https://gov.uk/service-manual

Wikiguías (Mexico)

The Wikiguías are a series of recommendations for implementing standardised digital services on Mexico's single government website gob.mx. The content consists of the framework for contributing to the single government website as well as the guidelines for implementing according to the provisions of Mexico's Digital Services Standard.

Source: https://www.gob.mx/wikiguias

Governance, spending and assurance

The *Recommendation of the Council on Digital Government Strategies* (OECD, 2014[1]) identifies that when it comes to digital government strategies countries should "establish effective organisational and governance frameworks to co-ordinate the implementation of the digital strategy within and across levels of government". Such an approach is also valuable in the context of designing and delivering services and builds on the development of style guides and guidance. This section will consider the importance of business cases and budget thresholds, procurement and commissioning activity, and service standards and assurance processes in enabling the design and delivery of services.

Because government consists of hundreds of organisations delivering hundreds of services, it is impossible for one organisation to manage the design and delivery of all those things directly. As a result, it is essential that countries establish a clear definition of 'good' in respect of services and develop a credible approach to quality assurance. Such governance models need to be built around identifying clear coordination responsibilities complemented by visibility and controls covering spending and delivery activity associated with digital and technology interventions.

Business cases and budget thresholds

The *Recommendation of the Council on Digital Government Strategies* (OECD, 2014[1]) identifies business cases as a critical element in securing the sustainability of digital government approaches through ensuring funding is available. Part of this exercise is to ensure a clear value proposition for all projects that can identify economic, social and political benefits as well as a process that involves all actors throughout government to ensure buy in and recognition of those benefits.

In the context of designing and delivering services such business case processes have important echoes of the need to carry out the research to understand a set of users, their needs and the potential ways in which government might respond. The business case and approval process needs to find ways to encourage experimentation by making funding available for research and prototype activities through a process that is lighter weight and less cumbersome than what might be expected for a full project implementation. Moreover, with an agile approach anticipating a continuous iteration of a service it is important for business case and funding processes to anticipate the need for delivery approaches that are continuously learning and as a result may pivot away from the original proposal having better understood the problem on an ongoing basis.

In the **United Kingdom**, a very early decision by the Government Digital Service was to make it possible for departments and agencies to carry out discovery and alpha activity without the need for a HM Treasury business case (HM Treasury and Government Finance Function, 2014[25]). In **France**, the team at beta.gouv.fr have developed a similar 'pre-incubation' phase where funding is available for teams to scope a problem and demonstrate the potential for a response without requiring a business case (beta.gouv.fr, n.d.[26]). The advantage of this approach to meeting well understood needs rather than spending time and energy on responding to assumed, but mistaken, needs can be seen in the way in which the **United Kingdom** developed GOV.UK Notify, as discussed in Box 2.14.

Box 2.14. How the discovery and alpha process helped GOV.UK Notify to meet user, not assumed, needs

Waiting to hear back from government as to whether an application has been processed or a decision has been made can cause anxiety. Not knowing the status of a particular outstanding request often leads people to pick up the phone and contact the relevant organisation to find out. In the UK for example, the Driver and Vehicle Licensing Agency would receive 2.4 million phone calls a year just for checks on the status of an application.

Given the cost this introduces for government and citizens this was an obvious contender for the UK's Government as a Platform programme to develop a status tracking platform as a common component. However, no work in the UK's digital agenda takes place without first completing a Discovery phase.

The starting point for this discovery was the desire to improve how government could keep people updated when they have made a request of government and the intent was to make it as easy as possible for service teams to keep users informed and so they interviewed teams and users from across government to establish their needs.

The most important thing the team did through this Discovery phase was validate the need for this problem to be solved. They found a huge demand across services for notifications from government - whether that's a receipt, a reminder, a request for something, or an update.

However, they also established that status tracking tools and platforms were not the immediate priority. Instead, they tested a hypothesis that well timed, proactive notifications from services would remove the majority of needs for status tracking tools. Telling people automatically about where an application or decision was in its workflow would reduce the need to pick up the phone. They found that one team in the Department for Work and Pensions was able to reduce unnecessary calls by 40% simply by sending people an email to say that their application had been received.

Although status tracking appeared to be the obvious solution the team's research showed that they are really "channel shift for anxiety" and solve a symptom rather than the problem. Although there is convenience in looking up the status this approach places a burden on the user to reach the point where they are worried rather than finding ways for services to communicate what they already know.

As a result, instead of considering the need to build both a status tracking platform and improved ways for teams to send notifications, the team was able to validate the real need and identify a more straightforward approach to delivery that could be implemented more quickly and with less overhead. The discovery also identified the importance to citizens of not only text messages and emails but physical letters too, developing the offering beyond what they had initially imagined. Internally, their understanding of public servant needs in relation to the back office system landscape meant that whilst automatic notifications were recognised as the ideal, the reality meant staff needed to have less technical way of sending notifications directly without a technical integration.

Source: Government Digital Service (2015[27]) *Gov, where's my stuff?*; Government Digital Service, (2016[28]), *Status tracking – making it easy to keep users informed*

Complementing business case processes are the ways in which countries invoke greater scrutiny of data, digital and technology spending when it reaches a particular budgetary threshold. That threshold can range from 10 000 EUR in **Portugal** to as high as 1 300 000 EUR in **Denmark.** These 'spend control' processes have become a feature where countries are developing the maturity of the broader public sector and seeking to shift particular approaches to procurement and formed part of previous recommendations made to Chile focusing on governing digital government (OECD, 2016[12]).

With the necessary mandate, such tools can enforce particular ways of working in terms of delivery methodologies or the re-use of common components whilst also providing a broad perspective on activity across government to help avoid duplication and increase the potential for collaboration on cross-government services that involve multiple actors. One important element in being able to create a far-sighted view on contractual break points and expiry dates as well as ongoing planning is to develop a pipeline of intended procurement. **Denmark, Norway**, **Portugal** and the **United Kingdom** are using this policy lever to improve the coherence and sustainability of investment, enforce the use of policy guidelines and standards and ensure any investment activity avoids any gaps or overlaps in delivery.

Procurement and commissioning

Whilst it is important to shape the way in which business cases are developed and spending approved it is also critically important to ensure that procurement and commissioning activities support the overall ambitions of service design and delivery across all relevant channels. The *Recommendation of the Council on Digital Government Strategies* (OECD, 2014[1]) emphasises the importance of procurement as an enabling contributor to broader ambitions around digital transformation. The ICT Commissioning Thematic Groups of the Working Party of Senior Digital Government Officials (E-Leaders) has been developing its thinking around approaches that can support agile commissioning and the delivery of transformed outcomes through The ICT Commissioning Playbook (E-Leaders Thematic Group on ICT Commissioning and OECD, 2019[29]). It contains the 11 plays in Figure 2.6.

Figure 2.6. Thematic Group on ICT Commissioning – draft principles

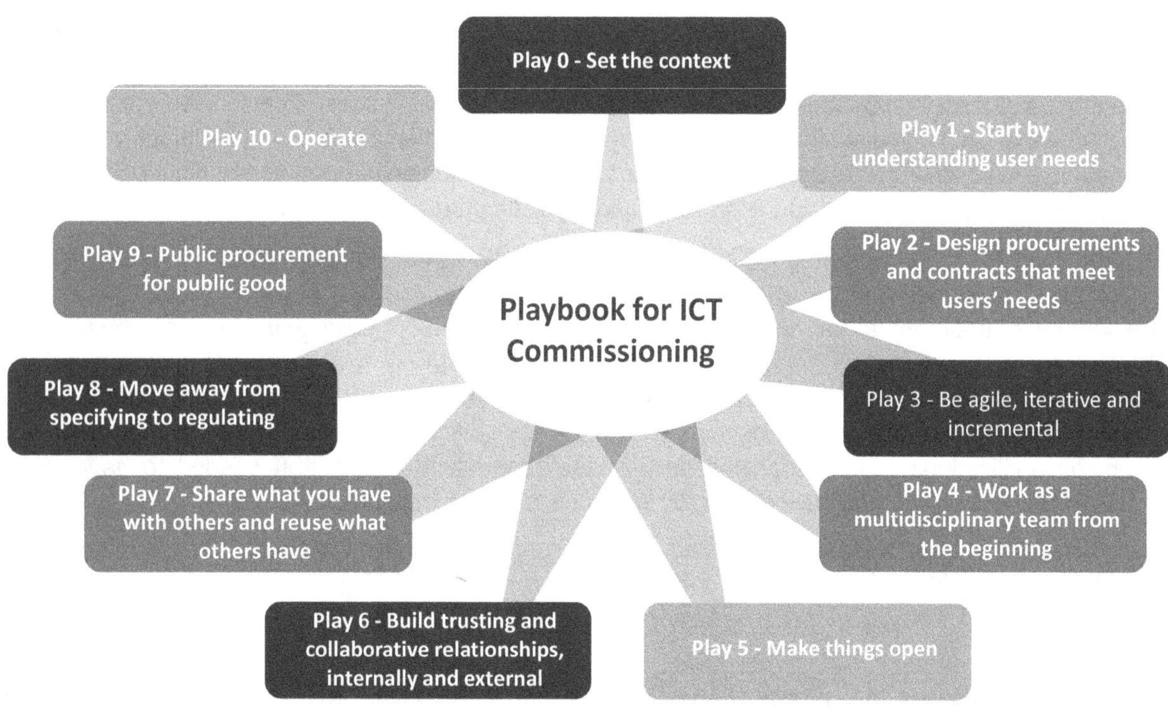

Source: E-Leaders Thematic Group on ICT Commissioning, (2019[29]) *The ICT Commissioning Playbook*

Procurement and commissioning that follow these principles can simplify the delivery of services while also affording opportunities to increase and develop the skills within the public sector too (see later section on public sector talent and skills) to ask the right questions of their suppliers. By changing the nature of how government engages suppliers this approach can shift the focus to outcomes and how all actors involved with designing and delivering services are challenged to respond to the needs of users. Furthermore, rethinking procurement activity can disrupt incumbent suppliers where inflexible contracts might stifle government's ability to respond to citizens.

The **United Kingdom** has adopted an approach, discussed in Box 2.15, that looks not only at how its Digital Marketplace has thought about the design of the frameworks shaping how goods are procured and commissioned but also at how expectations are set for suppliers through the Technology Code of Practice.

Box 2.15. Using procurement as a tool to transform services in the United Kingdom

The Technology Code of Practice

The Technology Code of Practice is a set of criteria that helps government design, build and buy technology. It is a cross-government agreed standard that supports the UK's spend controls process. As such, it informs the way in which business cases are developed by public servants. Because it is linked to the release of funding for delivering data, digital and technology projects it acts as a mechanism to influence the behaviours of any suppliers that are commissioned.

Source: Government Digital Service, (2016[30]) *Technology Code of Practice – GOV.UK*

Digital Marketplace frameworks

The aim of the Digital Marketplace is to make the commissioning of digital, data and technology projects and purchases simpler, clearer and faster. It does that by providing access to two frameworks: G-Cloud and Digital Outcomes and Specialists.

The G-Cloud framework provides a catalogue of cloud based goods and services – hosting, software and support. Between 2012 and 2018 GBP 4 billion of sales were reported with 45% of total sales by value, and 71% by volume, being awarded to small and medium-sized businesses.

The Digital Outcomes and Specialists (DOS) framework in contrast is not a catalogue in which suppliers can list their goods and buyers can browse to find what they need. Instead, the DOS framework is based on buyers explaining the situation they need addressing which is then published for eligible suppliers to see. These could be for achieving a particular outcome (for example, completing a discovery phase) or in sourcing specific specialist skills. Suppliers can then ask questions about the request and then, if they feel they can respond to it, propose a solution to meet the need. Between 2016 and 2018 almost GBP 800 million of sales were reported with 31% of total sales by value, and 82% by volume, being awarded to small and medium-sized businesses.

Source: Government Digital Service and Crown Commercial Service, (2019[31]), *G-Cloud framework sales (up to 31 December 2018)*; Government Digital Service and Crown Commercial Service, (2019[32]), Digital Outcomes and Specialists *framework sales (up to 31 December 2018)*

Standards and assurance processes

The power of a business case methodology in shaping the upfront behaviour of teams to ensure that they receive funding is clear and steps can be taken to influence the way in which procurement and commissioning is carried out. However, once that money is distributed the visibility of financial reporting will not necessarily provide confidence that the outcomes associated with the money will be in line with an overarching service design and delivery strategy.

One common response to this around the world has been for countries to establish a set of criteria against which the delivery and quality of services might be assessed. National standards for the design and delivery of standards exist in **Australia**[1], **Canada**[2], **Germany**[3], **Mexico**[4], **New Zealand**[5], **Singapore**[6], and the **United Kingdom**[7] whilst they have also been developed at different tiers and jurisdictions of government around the world.

Alongside the conceptual importance of establishing good in terms of outcomes as experienced by the public, governments can also take a view on the cross-government technical architecture to establish standards that can help to promote a consistent method for delivering within the public sector. Although not directly impacting on the user's experience of the services that are designed and delivered, the standards and attitudes around technology shape the ease with which innovation can be carried out and ensure that some of the most important enabling ideas, such as interoperability, are prioritised at an architectural level.

Some of these standards can be mandated centrally but the most effective approaches result from cross-government consensus about the opportunities and benefits of finding consistent approaches that allow for easier procurement and ensure guidance and best practices can be consolidated. These areas, as shown in Box 2.16 can cover quite diverse topics.

All these standards provide a common language for helping multiple delivery partners, whether public servants or suppliers, to work towards a shared ambition and according to agreed expectations of what good looks like. Nevertheless, it is important for the purposes of scrutiny, quality control and perhaps the ongoing release of funds, to establish appropriate assurance mechanisms that validate these standards are in place. One model is to create particular funding or delivery gateways associated with an increase in the quantity of users for whom the service is available (for example before a beta or before the live launch). An alternative is encourage ongoing relationships between the team responsible for controlling spend and the service delivery team so that assurance happens during the development of a service

Box 2.16. A selection of IT architectural and technology standards

IT Architecture Principles (Norway)

Assumed as common guidelines for all IT systems in the public sector, the principles are an important contribute to a common public sector architecture.

1. **Service orientation:** Functionality and performance level should be the main consideration in the development of IT solutions.
2. **Interoperability**: Platform should be able to interact with other platforms at an appropriate level.
3. **Availability**: Electronic services should be available when users need them, easy to find and user-friendly and universally designed.
4. **Safety**: IT solution itself and the information dealt must be protected in terms of confidentiality, integrity and availability, based on formal and risk-based requirements.
5. **Openness**: The methods and processes of IT solutions should be explained.
6. **Flexibility**: IT solutions should be designed in a way that minimizes the changes in work processes, content, organization, ownership and infrastructure.
7. **Scalability**: IT solutions must be able to be scaled as a consequence of changes in usage.
8. **References**: References should refer to regulations, circular, documents, etc.

Source: OECD, (2017[11]), *Digital Government Review of Norway: Boosting the Digital Transformation of the Public Sector*

The Common Public Digital Architecture (Denmark)

The common public framework architecture is built around 8 principles designed to help Danish public IT solutions be more interconnected and support usability, data sharing and cross-cutting processes in a secure and efficient way.

1. *Architecture is managed at the right level according to a common framework: significant architectural decisions are made as close to the task as possible.*

1. *Architecture promotes coherence, innovation and efficiency: the Common Public Framework architecture uses open standards with no binding to suppliers.*
2. *Architecture and regulation support each other: the architecture must support the fact that new legislation and regulation are digitally ready.*
3. *Security, privacy and trust are ensured: information security and privacy are incorporated into digital solutions.*
4. *Processes are optimised: digital solutions are developed across authorities with citizens and businesses as a starting point.*
5. *Good data is shared and reused: Concepts and data are described uniformly so that they can be reused and have a high quality.*
6. *IT solutions work together effectively: Digital solutions are built up so that they can interact with other organizations' digital systems.*
7. *Data and services are delivered reliably: The underlying infrastructure must meet agreed service objectives.*

Source: Digitaliseringsstyrelsen, (n.d.[33]), *Fællesoffentlig Digital Arkitektur*

Secure Cloud Strategy (Australia)

The Australian Digital Transformation Agency wants to make it easier for government to invest in cloud technologies as doing so can improve resilience, lift productivity and delivery better services. The Secure Cloud Strategy provides an analysis of the benefits available to public sector organisations for adopting cloud technologies and describes a framework for change to support all agencies, regardless of their stature, in making the transition.

Source: Digital Transformation Agency, (2017[34]), *Secure Cloud Strategy*

Open Source Contribution Policy (France)

In October 2016 France's law on the Digital Republic established an ambitious policy of promoting Open Source Software in the public sector. It prompted development of an Open Source Contribution Policy by the Inter-ministerial Directorate of Digital and the State Information and Communication System (*Direction Interministérielle du Numérique et du Système d'Information et de Communication de l'Etat*, DINSIC). The objectives of the policy are to:

- set the rules and principles for opening source codes
- support ministries and share good practice
- define the governance of contribution policies

Source: numerique.gouv.fr (2017[35]) *Politique de contribution aux logiciels libres de l'État*

Standards on APIs (Canada)

Application Programming Interfaces (APIs) provide an efficient and controlled way to make data accessible to other systems which promotes reuse and sharing of data and tooling. In Canada 10 standards have been identified to govern the development of APIs to better support integrated digital processes:

1. Follow the Government of Canada Digital Standards
2. Build robust RESTful APIs
3. Build well-defined and easy to consume message schemas
4. Consume what you build
5. Secure the API
6. Use consistent encoding and meta-data
7. Evolve and support the API throughout its lifecycle
8. Measure and publish API benchmarks
9. Use and design APIs sensibly
10. Publish and document the API

Source: Government of Canada (2019[36]), *Standards on APIs*

Digital inclusion

Digital divides are a significant obstacle to the successful and effective delivery of digital government strategies and in line with the *Recommendation of the Council on Digital Government Strategies* (OECD, 2014[1]) governments should take steps to address any digital divides that already exist and avoid the emergence of new forms of digital exclusion. This aspect of the Recommendation is a reaction to some of the unintended consequences of previous e-government activities. Arguably the ideal of 'digital by default' was never intended to mean the pursuit of online approaches to the exclusion of alternatives but in some cases that is exactly what has happened. In the rush to achieve the imagined benefits of channel shift and digitising existing analogue processes it can sometimes be forgotten that internet access is not ubiquitous, that populations lack the necessary skills and that online interactions are not always suitable for responding to the public service needs of the public.

In the context of designing and delivering services, it is critical to recognise that the journeys which a user takes to fulfil their need is not always going to be neatly contained within a phone call, a face to face exchange or an online transaction. Understanding the interplay between different channels and organisations from the initiation of the exchange through to its conclusion is central to good service design but it is also integral for responding to the challenge of addressing digital divides in society.

Digital literacy

Several of the service standards discussed earlier in this chapter acknowledge the importance of ensuring that design processes understand the context of users and lower barriers to usage. Adopting design led models for content and interaction patterns as well as structuring services in ways that make them usable by voice assistants and other AI powered tools mean that services become accessible, even for those who may not have the necessary literacy themselves.

One significant intervention in attempting to close the digital divide in terms of the inequality between those who may have access to the Internet or knowledge of its benefits, compared to those who do not, can be found through the way in which physical service locations have been used to offer training to the general public. In **Panama**, the *InfoPlazas* network operated by the National Secretariat of Science, Technology and Innovation (*Secretaría Nacional de Ciencia, Tecnología e Innovación*) and funded by the Inter-American Development Bank (IDB) (Banco Interamericano de Desarrollo, 2015[37]) offers training and builds knowledge for citizens to be able to take full advantage of online services (OECD, 2019[9]).

Therefore, while the use of technology and data can allow for proactive services that anticipate the needs of citizens to reduce friction, and service design practices can ensure services work are designed for all, complementary strategic efforts to increase digital literacy should not be forgotten.

Connectivity

One of the advantages of telephone based service provision over all channels is that it is usually possible to make a phone call (if not on mobile then on a landline) throughout a country. Physical locations necessarily suffer from geographic constraints whilst digital services can be put out of reach by limitations over coverage or affordability. Therefore, in thinking through the strategy for designing and delivering services, especially where there is an ambition for seamless experiences between telephone, physical and digital channels, it is critical to be aligned with those working on the question of connectivity in society both in terms of physical infrastructure but also in providing access to those who can't afford it themselves.

In **Mexico** (see Box 2.5), access to the internet has been recognised as a fundamental right, established in the Mexican constitution. Through *Mexico Conectado* internet access is being brought to 250,000 public spaces including hospitals, libraries, schools and government offices. In **Panama**, universal access to ICTs is also enshrined in law and led to the creation of the National Internet Network (*Red Nacional Internet*) covering 86% of the country and offering free access to the internet (OECD, 2019[9]).

Accessibility

A final aspect of digital inclusion concerns making sure that any service can be used by as many people as possible – including those with impaired vision, learning and motor difficulties and other disabilities. Some of these needs have been built into the physical environment for many years while telephone based services, particularly for those with hearing impairments, have also been developed. In **Chile**, a significant focus within ChileAtiende has been on the design of its settings to ensure that in person exchanges are as inclusive as possible. Online, some of those considerations can be overlooked and yet accessible websites and apps are better for all users – they often offer faster and easier to use or understand functionality.

An important aspect of service design is doing the research to ensure empathy with users and understanding their needs. This should extend to whether or not the service can be accessed. In the **United Kingdom**, the Government Digital Service has responded to this by developing an 'empathy lab' which can be used by others across government to use different digital assistive devices in order to understand the struggles a user might face (Government Digital Service, 2018[38]).

Although the World Wide Web Consortium (W3C) oversees international efforts to develop standards including the Web Content Accessibility Guidelines (WCAG) as part of the Web Accessibility Initiative (WAI)[8] they are not always mandated by law or enforced. Amongst the **European Union** countries the 2016 Web Accessibility Directive has increased the expectation over the importance of ensuring online public services and apps are accessible (Box 2.17).

Box 2.17. EU Web Accessibility Directive

Directive (EU) 2016/2102 came into force in December 2016. Its purpose is to provide people with disabilities with better access to websites and mobile apps used to deliver public services. The Directive:

- covers websites and mobile apps of public sector bodies, with a limited number of exceptions (e.g. broadcasters, live streaming);
- refers to specific standards to make websites and mobile apps more accessible. Such standards require for instance that there should be a text description for images, or that users are able to interact with a website without using a mouse, which can be difficult for some people with disabilities;
- requires the publication of an accessibility statement for each website and mobile app, describing the level of accessibility and indicating any content that is not accessible;
- calls for a feedback mechanism which the users can use to flag accessibility problems or to ask for the information contained in a non-accessible content;
- expects regular monitoring of public sector websites and apps by Member States, and that they report on the results of the monitoring. These reports have to be communicated to the Commission and to be made public for the first time by 23 December 2021.

Source: The European Commission (n.d.[39]), *Web Accessibility | Digital Single Market*

Channel strategy

The vision for a country's channel strategy in terms of providing access to a transformed experience of services is the responsibility of those with leadership roles, as discussed earlier in this chapter. However, the way in which different channels are designed and resourced plays a critical role in enabling teams to develop the services that can respond to the needs of their users with several examples discussed in Box 2.18.

The evolution of different channels in a country can leave behind a challenging legacy and a landscape of multiple channels. Although citizens might be able to access services via a website, over the phone, through a self-service kiosk in person they behave as separate siloes. This is the distinction between multi-channel and omni-channel approaches. In a multi-channel context interactions conducted online cannot then be followed up in person, issues raised over the phone are not trackable online and the services available through a self-service kiosk offer only a limited slice of functionality. With an omni-channel strategy the journey of a user is understood, and supported, across whichever channels they wish to use at whatever point in the journey they wish to access them and through whatever combination of services makes sense to their circumstances.

This returns to the importance of leadership in being able to ensure that there is a mandate for unifying service delivery brands across all of the channels identified in Figure 2.7 that might previously have operated as independent entities. While there is certainly a global trend towards consolidating all government websites into a single domain the real value of such an approach is in its potential for making sense of the full service landscape. As such, even before considering the enablers or channels best suited to the needs and practicalities of a given service it is fundamentally important to embed a philosophy of service design and delivery amongst those responsible for this agenda. Unless there is cross-government coordination and commitment to cut through organisational siloes and disrupt historic practices it will prove very hard to ensure a consistency of experience for the public.

Figure 2.7. Omni-channel services

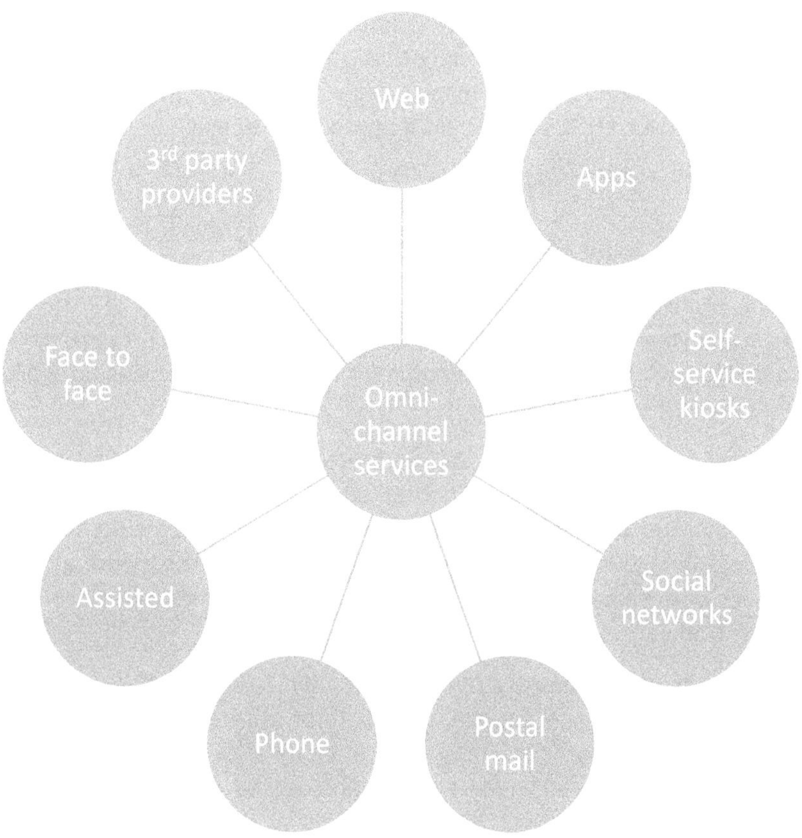

Box 2.18. Channels in Portugal, the Netherlands and the United Kingdom

Citizen shops, Citizen spots and ePortugal (Portugal)

Portugal's Administrative Modernisation Agency has the responsibility for a multi-channel approach to services. Operating physical locations, a call centre and the online channel, ePortugal, the focus is providing citizens with straightforward access to interactions with the state.

The first Citizen Shop opened in 1999 bringing together multiple public and private services into one location. Today there is a network of 56 locations, including a mobile venue, which have provided services to over 150 million citizens. This network is augmented by over 600 Citizen Spots that provide a point of access to approximately 200 services from different public sector entities allowing citizens to deal with a driving license, solve issues concerning employment, or change the address associated with their digital identity, among others. Some of these are co-located inside Citizen Shops but they are also found in many government buildings and post offices.

Alongside these physical locations, ePortugal streamlines the relationship between citizens, business owners and the Public Administration. This latest iteration of a single services website for Portugal was launched in 2019 and replaced the Citizen Portal, it is the primary channel for accessing information and providing public services. One of its features is Sigma, a virtual assistant that is also available through Facebook, which can quickly clarify queries, support navigation and carry out services such as changing an address. In contrast to the limited range of services available through face to face channels, ePortugal offers over 1500 services from around 580 entities.

Source: Administrative Modernisation Agency (AMA), (n.d.[40]), *Assistence*

Delivering local government without a town hall (Netherlands)

In January 2013 the municipality of Molenwaard was created following the merger of three local authorities. In the run up to this change the individual authorities had already merged their administrative operations but wanted to go further in terms of harmonising policy and processes whilst still being able to maintain closeness with their community.

In the event it was a discussion about where to build the new town hall that resulted in the Molenwaard Nearby. Facing a cost of 15 million € the council asked itself whether it needed to spend the money after all and, having digitalised its internal processes, decided to achieve greater flexibility and efficiency by operating 'virtual offices. Council staff do not have a fixed office; they work at home or at existing village halls, local clubs or even cafés in one of the municipality's thirteen villages or in a building where the local authority rents office space.

For the public, the majority of services are available electronically but where a physical interaction is required, for example for a driver's licence, passport or ID card, applications are handled by appointment with citizens choosing where they want to apply. The local authority goes out to where citizens or business are: the authority is mobile, digital and nearby.

When it comes to the democratic activity of the municipality then council meetings are also held at different locations.

Source: OECD Observatory of Public Sector Innovation, (2018[41]), *Providing municipal services without a town hall*

Helping users navigate between different channels (GOV.UK)

Every week millions of people use the UK government's GOV.UK website to do complex and sometimes life-changing tasks, such as learning to drive, getting a visa, or starting a business. Through ongoing user research and analysis of user journeys it became apparent that users were struggling to find what they needed in order to complete complex tasks.

The difficulty was that in order to complete the end to end process they would need to complete several tasks involving multiple pieces of content, accessing online services, obtaining physical forms or completing an offline step.

With these different steps owned by separate and siloed parts of government users had to piece the whole journey together themselves. Prior to the existence of GOV.UK the challenge would have been harder as users would have had to navigate multiple websites.

However, with GOV.UK being a single government domain it mean all content and transactions were hosted on the same site and could therefore be brought together and presented as simple, clear services. With all of the steps, whether content, transaction or offline, broken into easily manageable steps. While it sounds simple to achieve, this involved collaboration between multiple government departments to map the entirety of the end to end user journey recognising all the channels and interactions with government or third parties that might be involved.

As such, step-by-step navigation is more than a simple piece of additional functionality on GOV.UK it has become a model of collaborative workshops and re-usable design components, which means the process can be replicated for any government service.

More than 1.2 million users used the Learn to drive a car: step by step in its first 6 months and there are now over 30 step-by-step journeys live on GOV.UK, including some of most important and difficult tasks a user might ever need to do. These include:

- Employ someone: step by step
- Apply for a Standard visitor visa: step by step
- What to do when someone dies: step by step

The use of structured data means that these step-by-steps can be understood by search engines and voice assistants and used as a source of answers.

Source: OECD Observatory of Public Sector Innovation, (2018[41]), *GOV.UK step-by-step navigation*

Common components and tools

The conversation about digital in government can often assume that this is a technical problem requiring a technological solution. Historically, the e-government approach certainly encouraged this view of taking analogue processes and making them available online. To solve those problems means creating a shared set of enablers that look like websites, form builders and business process automation tools. However, such pieces of technology fail to account for the broader challenges of effecting the digital by design approaches that can transform outcomes for the public.

Technology in the form of common components and tools should be seen first as a means to supporting teams in meeting the needs of citizens rather than an end in themselves. Developing a 'Government as a Platform' ecosystem is about more than technology but enabling technology and platforms that can help teams respond to the needs of their users is a critical element of supporting the transformation of services.

This is particularly the case for those teams and areas of government responding to the 'long tail' of services. These are those processes that will never feature in the consciousness of politicians or organisational leadership because they may only consist of a handful of paper based transactions a week. Unlikely to be high profile they will not attract the resource to develop a transformed approach to the service and so they continue 'under the radar'. Individually these analogue or legacy e-government services are insignificant but collected together it is likely that there are significant quantities of services that could benefit from transformation. Making it possible for those parts of government that would otherwise never be able to transform the experience of their users is a critical driver for providing common components and tools. If this responsibility is picked up by a central function that can ensure there are strategic solutions to questions of identity for example, means that teams themselves can invest their energies in meeting the needs that are unique to their users.

Developing this platforms approach requires strategic thinking it is own right and the recently published Playbook: Government as a Platform (Pope, 2019[15]) provides an excellent guide for exploring the different aspects of developing, expanding and operating platforms within government. It covers:

- How to identify the users of your platforms and consider their needs
- How to identify the most relevant and appropriate platforms
- The importance of designing for self-service
- Data infrastructure, APIs and Open Standards
- Working across siloes
- Re-use of platforms within your own country but also internationally
- Funding and Operating platforms
- The elements involved in securing adoption of platforms
- The benefit to designing services of a platforms approach
- Identity, trust and consent

Answering the questions that these issues pose will ensure sustainable and viable approaches to support and provide a range of technical enablers such as hosting and infrastructure, low code and design systems, or digital identity, notifications and payments amongst others.

These elements are most valuable when working in combination. Through access to low code solutions, design systems, common components and hosting and infrastructure, service teams can deliver not only at pace and scale but with a level of quality and consistency of user experience that builds public trust and coherence amongst otherwise disparate public sector organisations. Box 2.19 explores how different enablers helped organisations in the **United Kingdom** to collaborate and quickly deliver new services to respond to the COVID-19 pandemic.

Hosting and infrastructure

Providing easy access to secure and scalable cloud infrastructure that reduces the demand for expensive web operations skills and simplifies the provisioning effort involved with moving from prototype into beta and on into live services is an approach that has been adopted by the **United States of America**[9] and the **United Kingdom**[10]. This is particularly valuable for those teams working with the 'long tail' of services that might otherwise lack the resources to develop their infrastructure.

Low code and Design systems

Low code approaches allow small teams to build end to end services that can replace expensive and legacy systems. These visual interfaces make use of common components and do not require specialist software engineering skills. They have been particularly beneficial in local government contexts, such as Adur and Worthing Councils in the **United Kingdom** who have saved 200 000 GBP per year in software licence costs and a tripling of productivity among some teams (OECD Observatory of Public Sector Innovation, 2019[42]). Nevertheless, low code solutions need to be looked at with a critical eye, mindful that they may deliver a solution with the risk of vendor lock in and at the expense of code quality, performance or accessibility.

A complementary approach is to develop design systems of reusable User Interface components, design patterns, accessibly written code and guidance to support implementation that ensure service teams can build in a consistent fashion. Providing reliable user experiences like this can help to build trust in a government brand whilst also continuously benefitting from the input of those teams that are researching and learning about its effectiveness in their use of its elements without being tied to the specifics of a given technology or contractual provider. Some examples of government design systems are those of **Argentina**[11], **Australia**[12], **Brazil**[13], **Canada**[14], **Singapore**[15], the **United States of America**[16], and the **United Kingdom**[17].

At their best, low code solutions should build on and incorporate the elements of these common design systems as well as platforms such as those discussed in the next section. Rather than a new team needing to address all the technical overheads involved in building a service from scratch, or carrying out user research on each element, this approach allows all teams, but particularly smaller ones with limited resources to piece together a full service, focusing their efforts on the overall service journey.

Digital Identity, Notifications, and Payments

A third area of common components and tools is that which is most commonly associated with Government as a Platform thinking, the specific platforms for digital identity, sending notifications and taking payments as well as others.

In the case of Digital Identity the OECD's report (OECD, 2019[43]) identified and compared the models being explored in **Austria**, **Canada**, **Denmark**, **Estonia**, **Italy**, **Korea**, **Norway**, **Portugal**, **Spain**, the **United Kingdom**, and **Uruguay**. Providing identity as a service to citizens and businesses that allows them to be verified in accessing digital services can be transformational in terms of obviating the need for physical documents and face to face interactions.

A second area is that of electronic notifications. In **Norway** residents have access to a digital mailbox while the example of GOV.UK Notify in the **United Kingdom** has been discussed in Box 2.14. Interestingly in the case of GOV.UK Notify the open source codebase has made it possible for **Canada** and **Australia** to reuse it in implementing their own common platforms for notifications.

Finally, payments is another area where countries are developing their own platforms with pagoPA in **Italy**[18] and GOV.UK Pay in the **United Kingdom**[19].

In **India**[20], the Aadhaar identity service has evolved into IndiaStack, providing a set of APIs for government and business to offer access to a universal biometric digital identity, paperless personal records, a single interface for cashless transactions, and a consent layer allowing data to move freely and securely.

Box 2.19. Enablers in action: responding to COVID-19 in the United Kingdom

The COVID-19 pandemic has completely changed daily life. The need for society to isolate as well as offsetting demand on health services has emphasised the role of digital in shifting away from physical interactions. In this situation, the service design and delivery foundations developed in the **United Kingdom** have been critical in enabling the fast and effective design and delivery of services demonstrating the breadth of how 'Government as a Platform' approaches can be understood throughout the public sector, and not simply in the context of centrally provided government services.

Content and services on GOV.UK

The most famous example of the UK's Government as a Platform approach is the single domain, GOV.UK. It is a single, trusted, and immediately known point of reference through which government can disseminate information and members of the public can access services.

Embedding live press conferences and clear medical messaging, www.gov.uk/coronavirus provided a single place through which to access all of the government's activity. The content was produced, and iterated, by teams in many organisations but unified under the GOV.UK brand. This also included access to services such as '*Offer coronavirus (COVID-19) support from your business*' or '*Find out what you can do if you're struggling because of coronavirus (COVID-19)*'. Each was published in its own open source code repository using the Design System, meaning teams could re-use accessible, user researched patterns with confidence the new services would work for users, and hosted on GOV.UK Platform as a Service, avoiding the need of standing up new infrastructure but instead immediately turning to a robust, secure and scalable solution. In one case, a member of the Government Digital Service reported going from initial commit to live service in 10 business hours.

Source: GOV.UK (n.d.[44]), *Coronavirus (COVID-19): what you need to do* (www.gov.uk/coronavirus); Government Digital Service (n.d.[45]), *alphagov/govuk-coronavirus-find-support: Helps citizens find out what help they can get during the COVID-19 pandemic* (https://github.com/alphagov/govuk-coronavirus-find-support); Government Digital Service (n.d.[46]), *alphagov/govuk-coronavirus-business-volunteer-form: Lets businesses volunteer with the response to the COVID-19 pandemic* (https://github.com/alphagov/govuk-coronavirus-business-volunteer-form); Towers, Richard (2020[47]), *https://twitter.com/RichardTowers/status/1243904365506760709*

Scaling GOV.UK Notify

GOV.UK Notify helps teams to send emails, text messages and letters to users and is available for central government, local authorities, or the NHS. With the COVID-19 pandemic prompting an ever greater need for simple tools to communicate with the public and within the public sector, GOV.UK Notify saw almost 500 new services launched between mid-February and mid-April 2020.

The experience of GOV.UK Notify highlights the importance of developing common components in the expectation of needing to scale to meet the needs of government, possibly overnight. This means designing a resilient technical architecture that can handle a dramatic increase in throughput, in this case going from a daily average of 1.4m emails and 150 000 SMS between mid-February and mid-March to a new average of 5m emails and 400 000 SMS between mid-March and mid-April. It also means starting from the premise of 'self-service' so that a new service can launch without training or the several layers of bureaucratic approval. GOV.UK Notify helps to achieve this with a freemium pricing model where charges only start after sending 250,000 text messages or wanting to send postal correspondence.

Source: Government Digital Service, (n.d.[48]), *[ARCHIVED CONTENT 20200208] GOV.UK Notify* (https://webarchive.nationalarchives.gov.uk/20200208053814/https://www.notifications.service.gov.uk/); Government Digital Service (n.d.[49]), *GOV.UK Notify* (https://www.notifications.service.gov.uk/); Government Digital Service (n.d.[50]), *Dashboard - GOV.UK Notify* (https://www.gov.uk/performance/govuk-notify)

Code sharing and collaboration between local authorities

Many public services will be accessed through local and municipal government and the COVID-19 pandemic has brought to the fore the power of inter-organisational networks to support collaboration, the role of open source code to make it easy for different public sector organisations to share and re-use solutions, and the important contributions that can be made by suppliers.

The London Borough of Camden initially worked with their supplier to develop the '*Get help if you're staying at home because of coronavirus*' service, including making the code openly available. Doing this allowed for its subsequent and rapid adoption by Buckinghamshire Council.

Elsewhere in the UK, local authorities including Croydon Council, Adur and Worthing Councils and Cumbria County Council have worked together using a common low-code platform to build, and then share, solutions for volunteer co-ordination, business grants management, workforce monitoring and workforce emergency alerts.

Source: Camden Council (n.d.[51]), *Get help if you're staying at home due to coronavirus* (https://coronavirus-help.camden.gov.uk/); Buckinghamshire Council (n.d.[52]), *Get help if you're staying at home due to coronavirus* (https://directory.buckinghamshire.gov.uk/); *FutureGov* (n.d.[53]), *wearefuturegov/coronavirus-service-directory: Simple service directory for local government coronavirus response* (https://github.com/wearefuturegov/coronavirus-service-directory); *Netcall* (n.d.[54]), *COVID-19 low-code applications for the public sector* (https://www.netcall.com/events/covid-19-package/)

Data-driven public sector

Transformed services are hard to achieve without a strategic approach to the role of data in the public sector. *The path to becoming a data-driven public sector* (OECD, 2019[55]) builds on the instruction of the *Recommendation of the Council on Digital Government Strategies* (OECD, 2014[1]) to "create a data-driven culture in the public sector". It provides a framework for countries and public sector organisations to use as the basis for identifying, and then responding to the challenges and opportunities of data-driven government to create a holistic, coherent and effective strategy for data that covers data governance, its application to generate value and the contribution it can make to strengthening trust in government.

In terms of data governance the OECD's model (Figure 2.8)) indicates strategic, tactical and operational areas of focus to ensure data-driven government. From this perspective, the elements of the model should be taken into consideration as a sub-layer of any public service design and delivery efforts, so that the value of data can be maximised.

In unlocking the potential for data-driven transformation of services, it is imperative that questions of implementation capacity (in terms of talent, stewardship and institutional leadership) and regulation (in terms of regulatory barriers and streamlined data access and sharing practices) are addressed. This will ensure that data flows steadily within government, across sectors and borders when needed, and always under the conditions to support trust.

Doing the hard work to solve the challenges of data sharing is important to unlocking services that are so good citizens are delighted to use them. Furthermore, at the technical level, it is important that data infrastructure and data architecture are prioritised to simplify the means by which services can access the needed data and instil confidence that when they do the quality is assured. Indeed, securing the quality and integrity of data across the value cycle (Figure 2.9) is essential for governments to have confidence in their innovations around the use of emerging technologies like Artificial Intelligence that can provide transformative benefits to the quality and scope of services provided by governments (Ubaldi et al., 2019[56]).

Figure 2.8. Data governance in the public sector

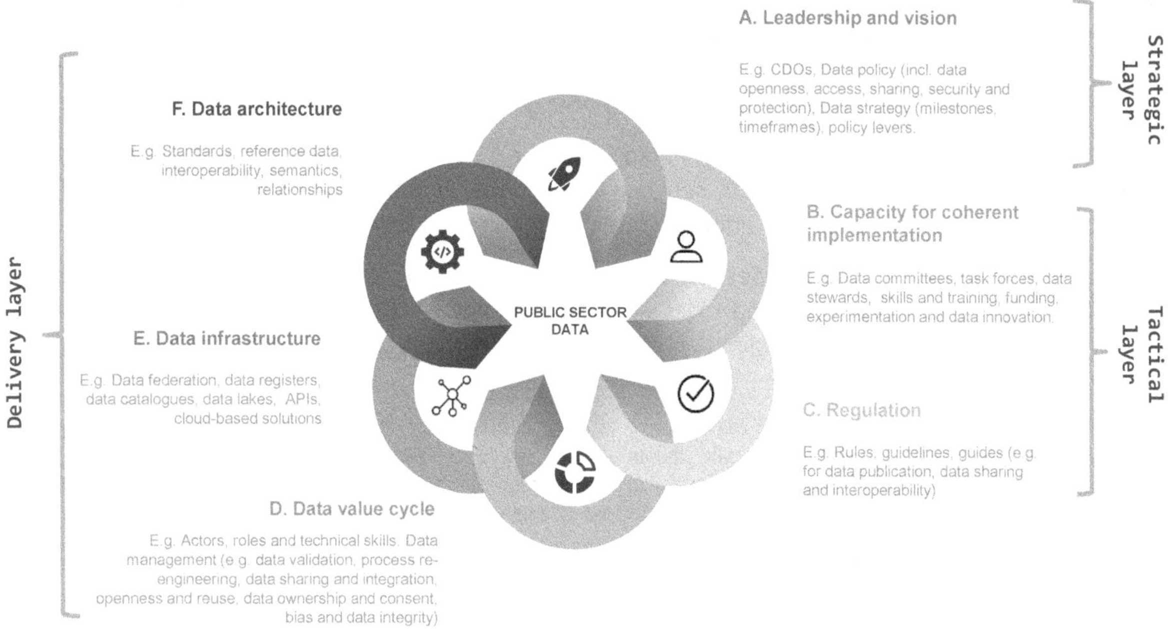

Source: OECD (2019[57]), *Digital Government Review of Argentina: Accelerating the Digitalisation of the Public Sector*

With those foundations in place it becomes possible to innovate in the design of data-driven services. Instead of simply replacing analogue processes, the more sophisticated use of data in services allows for them to be reimagined and for value to be brought both to providers of the services (i.e. public sector organisations) and users too. The design and delivery of services should recognise the opportunities to understand and apply data throughout the Government Data Value Cycle (Figure 2.9). In so doing delivery teams will begin to understand the potential for applying data in the anticipating and planning, delivery, and evaluation and monitoring of services.

Figure 2.9. The government data value cycle

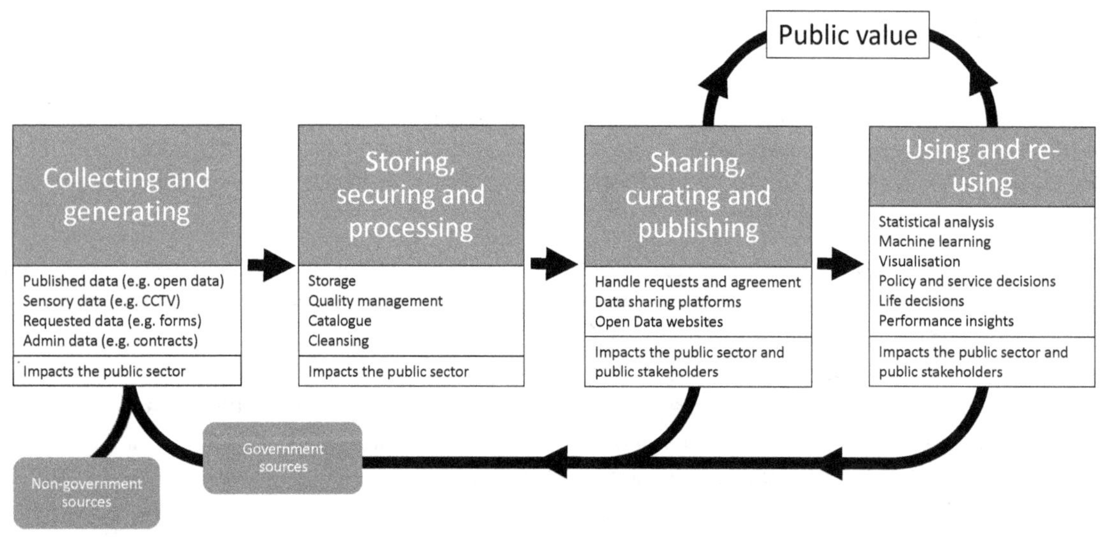

Source: van Ooijen, C., B. Ubaldi and B. Welby, (2019[58]), *A data-driven public sector: Enabling the strategic use of data for productive, inclusive and trustworthy governance*

Data are an important resource for teams in the planning of services providing quantitative and qualitative insights into the needs of users and the future permeations of a given policy. Moreover, it is imperative that data continue to be valued and understood in improving the delivery of a service and its monitoring over time. The ability for services to improve continuously in response to feedback and data about usage is essential in ensuring that the needs of users continue to be prioritised and met. In the **United Kingdom**, real-time service performance data are made available through public dashboards[21].

Understanding the performance of a service may benefit from mapping the flows of data across government. However, to achieve this a register of services may first be required. This can be a very simple concept and at its most basic simply list government services (such as examples from **Portugal**[22] and **Belgium**[23]). Greater sophistication may include the collection of contact details for the Senior Responsible Owner of a given service. This creates a transparency within government and a reference point for any concerns, questions or feedback about the experience of using it, thus facilitating the sharing of experiences and scaling up of good practices.

Such an approach paves the way for the possibility of such an index allowing for the simplification and rationalisation of government by bringing together the associated parts of government which are involved in administering the end to end experience of a user. An index of services therefore provides a tool with which to understand and map user journeys.

In terms of the experience of accessing services, a data-driven public sector is not only proactive in innovating around the services that citizens access but effective in ensuring that citizens do not need to provide government with information that it already knows about them. This *Once Only Principle* is increasingly evident amongst OECD countries with **Estonia** providing leadership in this area and making it a legal obligation in 1997 and following it up with the resources to subsequently develop national interoperability infrastructure (OECD, 2015[5]).

Of equal importance to the experience of external users is ensuring that service design and delivery teams are aware of data resources and equipped to make the most of them. Finding ways, such as through a catalogue of services, base data registries and APIs, to ensure teams are able to find out what data are available and what attributes can be established without asking the user again is valuable. Particular datasets that can be used to develop services should also be easy to find. The OpenFisca project[24], initiated by **France** but now containing the tax and benefit systems of eight countries including **Italy**, **New Zealand**, **Tunisia**, and **Uruguay** provides access to the underlying rules of government as code that can be used, and re-used to build more effective services (see Box 2.20 for more detail on 'Rules as Code').

Where data are being applied throughout the delivery lifecycle it is imperative that questions of trust are considered within the design of the service. Exploring the relevant trust implications of ethics, transparency, consent and security is a critical dimension to ensure that any services build the confidence of their audience rather than jeopardising their trust.

Box 2.20. Rules as Code

The OpenFisca initiative discussed above is a technical response to the idea of 'Rules as Code'. It provides an open source platform for modelling legislation (and rules) in code to improve the transparency of, and access to, the law.

This is one component of the broader 'Rules as Code' idea, which is less about technology and is instead more about changing the way in which government approaches one of its core activities: rulemaking. Government rules are found in a variety of places including legislation, regulations or policy documents, but are not produced in ways that can be readily consumed by machines.

The 'Rules as Code' movement is a reaction to the analogue nature of the systems that underpin the production of government rules, and an effort to address several of the problems that these systems cause. At its simplest 'Rules as Code' anticipates that government rules (legislation, policy, business rules) could be created in such a way that they could be consumed by machines (namely, computers).

This represents a significant departure from the status-quo of how governments create rules and instead calls on governments to integrate established and new technologies into the rule creation process. Current thinking proposes three ways of conceptualising 'Rules as Code':

1. As an output: the result is a version of the rules in code that can then be understood and used by a computer.
2. As an approach, as well as an output: the result changes the process of drafting legislation, regulation and policy to enable the creation of rules that can be read and used by computers. Conceptualised in this way, it is about changing *when*, *how*, *by* and *for whom* rules are made.
3. As a fundamental restructuring of the rule creation process: machine-consumable versions of legislation, regulation and policy are part of the initial drafting stage rather than produced at its end. This means authoritative, machine-consumable version of rules being produced by governments for third party consumption not through the efforts of individual end-users.

Source: Mohun, Roberts and Amaral (Forthcoming[59]), *Cracking the Code: Rule-making for machines and humans*

Public sector talent and capabilities

The people who make up the teams that design and deliver services are crucial to the success of efforts to better meet the needs of the public. However, with the digital government and service design model representing a paradigm shift in practice it can be the case that government does not have the necessary talent and capabilities within its organisation and faces significant constraints in terms of their acquisition. This area is an increasing priority for the Working Party of Senior Digital Government Officials (E-Leaders) and in 2020 will see a new Thematic Group established to share best practices and support one another in addressing this area.

In terms of establishing the 'Government as a Platform' ecosystem that can support teams in designing and delivering services this section will explore five areas in which public sector talent and capabilities need to be thought about and developed. They are: skills and training, recruitment and job families, professions and their communities of practice, consultancy and coaching, and finally skills transfer.

Skills and training

The starting point for any analysis of the public sector talent and capability must be with the existing staff and team members who have been working in and around the design and delivery of services. This includes those who have worked in policy roles, delivery roles and operationally as the ambition is to create multi-disciplinary teams that understand the breadth of the user's experience. Carrying out such an audit will help to identify those with an eagerness to branch out into digital government and service design roles and help support those for whom different roles might be better.

Where new training is needed, or a change of role more suitable there is a danger that such a move confirms the fears people have that the digital agenda is a threat to jobs and exacerbate tensions with unions who equate digital government with an inevitable loss of jobs. It is true that every time an analogue process is removed or a data-driven proactive exchange of information is introduced that happens at the expense of a previous manual task. Nevertheless, this provides an opportunity to explore retraining opportunities for those who are affected and work with unions to offset risks by including them as part of embedding a new digital and service design led culture in government.

Several OECD countries, including **Italy** and the **United Kingdom** have developed particular curriculums and training programmes that speak to the need to equip their staff with the necessary skills to support the digital and service design agenda. In the **United Kingdom**, the ambition of the Digital Academy is to create a critical mass of staff working at every grade throughout the public sector having confidence when it comes to digital, data and technology awareness.

Recruitment

Taking a service design approach to the delivery of services may require the reshaping of roles required to meet the needs of citizens. Whilst it may be possible to retrain long-standing members of staff there will be a capability gap that needs to be addressed through recruitment. However, with new roles comes the challenge of identifying the appropriate pay and conditions to be competitive with the market whilst operating within the constraints of the existing public sector pay arrangements.

Those constraints may make it impossible to bring digital government skills in-house immediately. Therefore, when faced with a lag in terms of retraining the existing workforce and challenges in terms of recruiting new staff, it will be necessary to work with the supplier ecosystem to explore ways of bringing in particular specialisms. This may necessitate the creation of special procurement frameworks or working with Human Resource colleagues to find flexibility in securing the necessary leadership, talent and capabilities on which to start developing the service design agenda. It is important to ensure that any service design and digital government agenda that has aspirations for transforming the way citizen and state interact makes the necessary commitment to accessing the skills required for it to be achieved.

Job families, professions and their communities of practice

A further important step is to recognise the longer-term realignment of job families and recruitment parameters. Working with Human Resource colleagues and those responsible for the structure of jobs and roles across the public service provides the opportunity to think about and define the job families needed to support digital, data and technology professionals. While many governments will have ICT functions and a track record in technology and e-government disciplines these may not be fit for purpose in terms of their roles such as Web Operations Engineers, User Research, Product Management and Service Design as well as others. Moreover, it will be necessary to identify the expected career path for these roles and be conscious of the steps that might be needed in order to retain or replace staff.

Having understood the skills of the workforce, identified the disciplines required and started to evolve recruitment practices and design the necessary career paths the next element in developing a cross-government environment that can support service design and delivery is to designate the necessary leadership of those professions and begin to develop cross-government communities. The **United Kingdom**'s experience in developing a profession and communities of practice is in Box 2.21.

Consultancy and coaching

One of the challenges with questions of talent and capability in the service design and delivery agenda is how you scale these skills and abilities throughout the entirety of government at the pace that's needed to embed this paradigm shift. Whilst suppliers working according to the standards and assurance processes discussed earlier can be part of the solution the value of consultancy and coaching should not be neglected.

In **Chile**, the GobLab provides an excellent model for how such consultancy might look. While ostensibly providing a service to partners across the public sector, the interactions between GobLab and their clients has a coaching element. Therefore, as a centre of excellence is developed and different professions become more established throughout the public sector there is a valuable opportunity to be exploited in providing 'consultancy' services out to colleagues across government whilst at the same time investing in the skills of the organisation with whom the work is being carried out.

Skills transfer

The final area in which public sector talent and capability can be an enabler for teams working to meet the needs of their users is through the relationships that are developed with suppliers. Historically teams might have identified a set of requirements, run a procurement exercise and outsourced the delivery of the solution to an off-site team that was managed as part of a contract rather than there being any co-delivery. According to the philosophies of service design discussed in terms of co-working, collaboration and iterative development a different model of working with suppliers is necessary.

As such, procurement exercises that focus on outcomes rather than specifications for a delivered solution can provide an opportunity to specify knowledge transfer skills. In the initial exchanges with the supplier the responsibility might be for 100% of the delivery but, over time, if the expectation is part of the contracted outcome that should decrease as the public sector staff pick up more of the responsibility until there comes a point where the supplier is fulfilling a coaching role. At that point the necessary knowledge and capability has been internalised by the public sector organisation and the relationship with the supplier may no longer be needed.

Box 2.21. Leadership for transforming public sector talent and capability

The Digital, Data and Technology Profession is a specific team within the Civil Service human resource structure that helps all government departments to attract, develop and retain the people and skills they need to achieve government transformation.

Their work covers workforce insights and analytics, career management, pay and reward, communities of practice, learning and development, attraction and recruitment, diversity and inclusion, and employer brand and culture. Their priorities cover five areas:

- enable workforce planning through the use of insights and analytics (this aspect of human resource management forms the basis for a case study included within The path to becoming a data-driven public sector (OECD, 2019[55]))
- bring consistency to job roles through a common capability framework
- work on more consistent approach towards pay and reward; create and develop communities of practice
- create training and development for digital, data and technology professions through the GDS Academy
- support the development of a diverse and inclusive culture.

The UK has an estimated 17 000 civil servants employed in digital, data and technology roles. The Capability Framework describes the 39 different job roles that the UK has identified in the Digital, Data and Technology Profession and provides details of the skills needed to work at each level of the role.

Communities of practice have grown up around each of the roles – the design community, the user research community, the content design community. These provide a network of practitioners that can support one another, share best practices, learn and continue to evolve the discipline in government. Each community is free to organise in the way that is best suited to their needs but there is a designated lead who coordinates activity across government and within departments too.

In the context of the UK's single government domain the content design community is particularly important. The GOV.UK editorial model is to have a core team of content designers responsible for high profile content but to then work with a distributed network of hundreds of editors who handle the content relating to their department or specialist users. ConCon (ContentConference) is an annual conference that brings together all the editors responsible for content on GOV.UK to share their experiences, to build relationships and to celebrate their successes together.

Source: Digital, Data and Technology Profession (n.d.[60]) *About us*; Digital, Data and Technology Profession (2017[61]), Digital, Data and Technology Profession Capability Framework

References

(n.a.) (n.d.), *Assistence - AMA*, https://www.ama.gov.pt/web/agencia-para-a-modernizacao-administrativa/atendimento (accessed on 13 December 2019). [40]

Banco Interamericano de Desarrollo (2015), *Programa de mejora de la competitividad y los servicios públicos a través del gobierno electrónico*, Banco Interamericano de Desarrollo, http://idbdocs.iadb.org/wsdocs/getdocument.aspx?docnum=40057894. [37]

Beck, K. et al. (2001), *Manifesto for Agile Software Development*, https://agilemanifesto.org/ (accessed on 17 April 2020). [22]

beta.gouv.fr (n.d.), *Le programme de préincubation*, https://beta.gouv.fr/preincubation/. [26]

Buckinghamshire Council (n.d.), *Get help if you're staying at home due to coronavirus*, https://directory.buckinghamshire.gov.uk/ (accessed on 16 April 2020). [52]

Camden Council (n.d.), *Get help if you're staying at home due to coronavirus*, https://coronavirus-help.camden.gov.uk/ (accessed on 16 April 2020). [51]

Commonwealth of Australia (2018), *I want to work, Employment Services 2020 Report*. [20]

Department of Jobs and Small Business (2018), *Employment Services 2020: Consultation report*. [18]

Digital Data and Technology Profession (2017), *Digital, Data and Technology Profession Capability Framework - GOV.UK*, https://www.gov.uk/government/collections/digital-data-and-technology-profession-capability-framework. [61]

Digital Data and Technology Profession (n.d.), *About us - Digital, Data and Technology Profession - GOV.UK*, https://www.gov.uk/government/organisations/digital-data-and-technology-profession/about. [60]

Digital Transformation Agency (2017), *Secure Cloud Strategy*, https://www.dta.gov.au/our-projects/secure-cloud-strategy. [34]

Digital.gov (n.d.), *Style Guides by Government Agencies / Digital.gov*, https://digital.gov/resources/style-guides-by-government-agencies/. [23]

Digitaliseringsstyrelsen (n.d.), *Principper og regler | Fællesoffentlig Digital Arkitektur*, https://arkitektur.digst.dk/principper-og-regler. [33]

Downe, L. (2019), *Good Services: How to Design Services that Work*, BIS PUBLISHERS B V. [13]

Downe, L. (2018), *15 principles of good service design*, https://blog.louisedowne.com/2018/06/14/15-principles-of-good-service-design/ (accessed on 24 January 2019). [14]

E-Leaders Thematic Group on ICT Commissioning and OECD (2019), *The ICT Commissioning Playbook*, https://playbook-ict-procurement.herokuapp.com/. [29]

European Commission (n.d.), *Web Accessibility | Digital Single Market*, https://ec.europa.eu/digital-single-market/en/web-accessibility. [39]

FutureGov (n.d.), *wearefuturegov/coronavirus-service-directory: Simple service directory for local government coronavirus response*, https://github.com/wearefuturegov/coronavirus-service-directory (accessed on 16 April 2020). [53]

GOV.UK (2016), *A to Z - Style guide - Guidance - GOV.UK*, https://www.gov.uk/guidance/style-guide/a-to-z-of-gov-uk-style. [24]

GOV.UK (n.d.), *Coronavirus (COVID-19): what you need to do*, https://www.gov.uk/coronavirus (accessed on 16 April 2020). [44]

Government Digital Service (2019), *What Service Communities are achieving across government*, https://gds.blog.gov.uk/2019/01/28/what-service-communities-are-achieving-across-government/. [21]

Government Digital Service (2018), *Creating the UK government's accessibility empathy lab*, https://gds.blog.gov.uk/2018/06/20/creating-the-uk-governments-accessibility-empathy-lab/. [38]

Government Digital Service (2016), *Status tracking - making it easy to keep users informed*, https://gds.blog.gov.uk/2015/10/05/status-tracking-making-it-easy-to-keep-users-informed/. [28]

Government Digital Service (2016), *Technology Code of Practice - GOV.UK*, https://www.gov.uk/government/publications/technology-code-of-practice. [30]

Government Digital Service (2015), *Gov, where's my stuff?*, https://gds.blog.gov.uk/2015/08/26/gov-wheres-my-stuff/. [27]

Government Digital Service (2012), *No link left behind*, https://gds.blog.gov.uk/2012/10/11/no-link-left-behind/. [6]

Government Digital Service (n.d.), *[ARCHIVED CONTENT 20200208] GOV.UK Notify*, https://webarchive.nationalarchives.gov.uk/20200208053814/https://www.notifications.service.gov.uk/ (accessed on 16 April 2020). [48]

Government Digital Service (n.d.), *alphagov/govuk-coronavirus-business-volunteer-form: Lets businesses volunteer with the response to the COVID-19 pandemic*, https://github.com/alphagov/govuk-coronavirus-business-volunteer-form (accessed on 16 April 2020). [46]

Government Digital Service (n.d.), *alphagov/govuk-coronavirus-find-support: Helps citizens find out what help they can get during the COVID-19 pandemic*, https://github.com/alphagov/govuk-coronavirus-find-support (accessed on 16 April 2020). [45]

Government Digital Service (n.d.), *Dashboard - GOV.UK Notify*, https://www.gov.uk/performance/govuk-notify (accessed on 16 April 2020). [50]

Government Digital Service (n.d.), *GOV.UK Notify*, https://www.notifications.service.gov.uk/ (accessed on 16 April 2020). [49]

Government Digital Service and Crown Commercial Service (2019), *Digital Outcomes and Specialists framework sales (up to 31 December 2018) - GOV.UK*, https://www.gov.uk/government/statistical-data-sets/digital-outcomes-and-specialists-framework-sales-up-to-31-december-2018. [32]

Government Digital Service and Crown Commercial Service (2019), *G-Cloud framework sales (up to 31 December 2018) - GOV.UK*, https://www.gov.uk/government/statistical-data-sets/g-cloud-framework-sales-up-to-31-december-2018. [31]

Government of Canada (2019), *Government of Canada Standards on APIs*, https://www.canada.ca/en/government/system/digital-government/modern-emerging-technologies/government-canada-standards-apis.html. [36]

HM Treasury and Government Finance Function (2014), *Agile digital and IT projects: clarification of business case guidance*, https://www.gov.uk/government/publications/the-green-book-appraisal-and-evaluation-in-central-governent/agile-digital-and-it-projects-clarification-of-business-case-guidance. [25]

Local Digital and Ministry of Housing Communities and Local Government (2018), *The Local Digital Declaration*, https://localdigital.gov.uk/declaration/. [3]

MINSEGPRES (2019), *Ley 21.180 de Transformación Digital del Estado*, https://www.leychile.cl/Navegar?idNorma=1138479 (accessed on 12 December 2019). [10]

Mohun, J., A. Roberts and M. Amaral (Forthcoming), "Cracking the Code: Rule-making for machines and humans", *OECD Working Papers on Public Governance*, OECD, Paris. [59]

Netcall (n.d.), *COVID-19 low-code applications for the public sector*, https://www.netcall.com/events/covid-19-package/ (accessed on 16 April 2020). [54]

numerique.gouv.fr (2017), *Politique de contribution aux logiciels libres de l'État*, https://www.numerique.gouv.fr/publications/politique-logiciel-libre/. [35]

OECD (2019), *Digital Government in Chile – Digital Identity*, OECD Digital Government Studies, OECD Publishing, Paris, https://dx.doi.org/10.1787/9ecba35e-en. [43]

OECD (2019), *Digital Government Review of Argentina: Accelerating the Digitalisation of the Public Sector*, OECD Publishing, Paris, https://doi.org/10.1787/354732cc-en (accessed on 24 June 2019). [57]

OECD (2019), *Digital Government Review of Panama: Enhancing the Digital Transformation of the Public Sector*, OECD Digital Government Studies, OECD Publishing, Paris, https://dx.doi.org/10.1787/615a4180-en. [9]

OECD (2019), *The Path to Becoming a Data-Driven Public Sector*, OECD Digital Government Studies, OECD Publishing, Paris, https://dx.doi.org/10.1787/059814a7-en. [55]

OECD (2017), *Digital Government Review of Norway: Boosting the Digital Transformation of the Public Sector*, OECD Digital Government Studies, OECD Publishing, Paris, https://dx.doi.org/10.1787/9789264279742-en. [11]

OECD (2017), *Government at a Glance 2017*, OECD Publishing, Paris, https://dx.doi.org/10.1787/gov_glance-2017-en. [7]

OECD (2017), *Recommendation of the Council on Open Government, OECD/LEGAL/0438*, OECD, Paris, https://legalinstruments.oecd.org/en/instruments/OECD-LEGAL-0438. [2]

OECD (2016), *Digital Government in Chile: Strengthening the Institutional and Governance Framework*, OECD Digital Government Studies, OECD Publishing, Paris, https://dx.doi.org/10.1787/9789264258013-en. [12]

OECD (2015), *OECD Public Governance Reviews: Estonia and Finland: Fostering Strategic Capacity across Governments and Digital Services across Borders*, OECD Public Governance Reviews, OECD Publishing, Paris, https://dx.doi.org/10.1787/9789264229334-en. [5]

OECD (2014), *Recommendation of the Council on Digital Government Strategies, OECD/LEGAL/0406*, OECD, Paris, https://legalinstruments.oecd.org/en/instruments/OECD-LEGAL-0406. [1]

OECD (n.d.), *Digital government toolkit - Mexico: National Digital Strategy*, https://www.oecd.org/gov/mexico-digital-strategy.pdf. [8]

OECD Observatory of Public Sector Innovation (2019), *Developing digital services using low code - Observatory of Public Sector Innovation*, https://oecd-opsi.org/innovations/developing-digital-services-using-low-code/. [42]

OECD Observatory of Public Sector Innovation (2018), *Design and implementation of a citizen centric employment services system - Observatory of Public Sector Innovation*, https://oecd-opsi.org/innovations/design-and-implementation-of-a-citizen-centric-employment-services-system/. [19]

OECD Observatory of Public Sector Innovation (2018), *GOV.UK step-by-step navigation - Observatory of Public Sector Innovation*, https://oecd-opsi.org/innovations/gov-uk-step-by-step-navigation/. [41]

OECD Observatory of Public Sector Innovation (2018), *Redesign of the Unique Certificate of Disability - Observatory of Public Sector Innovation*, https://oecd-opsi.org/innovations/certificado-unico-de-discapacidad-cud-redesign-of-the-granting-service-of-the-unique-certificate-of-disability/. [16]

OECD Observatory of Public Sector Innovation (2018), *The Local Digital Declaration - Observatory of Public Sector Innovation*, https://oecd-opsi.org/innovations/the-local-digital-declaration/. [4]

Pope, R. (2019), *Playbook: Government as Platform*, Ash Center for Democratic Governance and Innovation, Harvard University. [15]

Towers. Richard (2020), *Richard Towers on Twitter*, https://twitter.com/RichardTowers/status/1243904365506760709 (accessed on 16 April 2020). [47]

Ubaldi, B. et al. (2019), "State of the art in the use of emerging technologies in the public sector", *OECD Working Papers on Public Governance*, No. 31, OECD, Paris. [56]

van Ooijen, C., B. Ubaldi and B. Welby (2019), "A data-driven public sector: Enabling the strategic use of data for productive, inclusive and trustworthy governance", *OECD Working Papers on Public Governance*, No. 33, OECD, Paris. [58]

Welby, B. (2019), "The impact of Digital Government on citizen well-being", *OECD Working Papers on Public Governance*, No. 32, OECD, Paris. [17]

Notes

[1] https://www.dta.gov.au/help-and-advice/digital-service-standard/digital-service-standard-criteria

[2] https://www.canada.ca/en/government/system/digital-government/government-canada-digital-standards.html

[3] http://publicservicelab.de/Ressourcen/Deutschland-Servicestandard.pdf

[4] https://www.gob.mx/serviciosdigitales/es/articulos/principios-generales-de-diseno-de-servicios-digitales

[5] https://www.digital.govt.nz/standards-and-guidance/digital-service-design-standard/

[6] https://www.tech.gov.sg/digital-service-standards/

[7] https://www.gov.uk/service-manual/service-standard

[8] https://www.w3.org/WAI/

[9] https://cloud.gov

[10] https://www.cloud.service.gov.uk

[11] http://argob.github.io/poncho/

[12] https://designsystem.gov.au

[13] http://dsgov.estaleiro.serpro.gov.br/

[14] https://www.canada.ca/en/government/about/design-system.html

[15] https://designsystem.isomer.gov.sg

[16] https://v2.designsystem.digital.gov

[17] https://design-system.service.gov.uk/

[18] https://www.pagopa.gov.it/

[19] https://www.payments.service.gov.uk/

[20] https://indiastack.org/

[21] https://www.gov.uk/performance

[22] https://eportugal.gov.pt/servicos

[23] https://www.belgium.be/fr/services_en_ligne/overview

[24] https://openfisca.org/

3 The experience of Chile

This chapter presents a summary of service provision in Chile. It opens with a discussion of the background to services in Chile providing the origins and evolution of ChileAtiende into the service it provides today.
That status quo is presented in three parts: the oversight of services in Chile; the operation of ChileAtiende; and finally, an overview of the various other service delivery channels that exist in the country.

This chapter will consider the service design and delivery experience of Chile. To begin with, the chapter will present the origins of ChileAtiende and its evolution since then. Having traced its evolution, the chapter will consider the present status of service delivery in Chile with a discussion of both ChileAtiende and the other ways in which the public can access services.

Having described the current situation, this chapter will analyse the current situation in light of the conceptual framework advanced in the previous chapter in focusing on an analysis of the context, the philosophy and the enablers for service design and delivery in Chile.

The background to services in Chile

When the Piñera administration took office in 2010, it made the experience of citizens in accessing services a political priority. To do this the President created a Committee - led by the former Modernisation and Digital Government Unit (MDGU, now the Digital Government Division) at MINSEGPRES - tasked with improving the proximity of the state to citizens and the ease with which public services could be accessed. This mandate allowed the committee to coordinate service delivery across agencies, engaging each institution in turn and offering support with improving their service delivery.

From these exchanges, the multi-channel model of ChileAtiende emerged to provide a single point of access to government. Modelled on the experience of Canada in the design and delivery of Service Canada (see Box 3.1), the vision for this network of physical locations, a telephone call centre and a website was for citizens to be able to access all they needed in the same place across multiple government services and with visibility of their historic interactions with the state. Alongside the creation of this multi-channel network was the ambition to build a brand, and a concept, that resonated with the public and increased adoption of services through the most appropriate channel.

Box 3.1. Service Canada

The inspiration for ChileAtiende drew on several international examples including eCitizen in Singapore, Centrelink in Australia and Service Canada to be from the outside a network of provision across multiple channels and not just an online, e-government approach to meeting the needs of the public.

Service Canada was one of the inspirations because it has an impressive pedigree in wanting to meet the needs of Canadians. In 1998, the government undertook detailed surveys of citizens' needs and expectations to develop "an integrated citizen-centred service strategy". Yet it was not until 2005 that Service Canada formally began operations with a mandate to offer a single point of access to a wide range of government services and benefits through the Internet, by telephone, in person or by mail.

To fulfil this responsibility Service Canada has 610 locations across the 13 provinces and territories of the country with further mobile outreach services operating in remote and isolated areas. Online, Service Canada provides access to more than 72 government programs and services (Canada.ca, 2019[1]).

Service Canada recently opened a new flagship location designed with their users at its heart and acting as a testing ground for future innovations to be rolled out nationally. This includes the availability of virtual based service delivery increasing the availability of services by introducing access to offsite members of staff with particular specialisms. This understanding of the importance of moving from in-person to online is underscored by providing tablets, headsets and public Wi-Fi to encourage their visitors to self-serve where possible. The flagship location has also introduced innovations to support those who access services with the assistance of inclusive technologies putting a high priority on accessibility for all.

The Service Canada team also looks to enhance the accessibility of its services with those who are located outside the scope of their physical locations. The Satellite-in-a-Suitcase project for example is designed to bring connectivity to Canadians in remote communities. Given the geographic context of Canada there is a challenge of creating the necessary connectivity to ensure access to services. In response to the need Service Canada developed a solution that equips their outreach staff with the necessary mobile technology to connect to the same experience as those who visit any Service Canada Centre.

Source: Canada.ca, (2019[2]), *Improving services for Canadians*

The means by which this vision was put into reality was through integrating two existing service delivery channels: Chile's original e-government platform, *ChileClick*; and the physical network operated by the Social Security Institute (*Instituto de Previsión Social*, IPS) to administer the state pension. When reforms to the social security system reduced demand for IPS services (see Figure 3.1), its network of physical locations was combined with *ChileClick* to support a multi-channel strategy in order reduce the time and effort involved for citizens in visiting multiple locations for their needs of government to be met. This hybrid of physical and online channels would eventually become ChileAtiende.

Figure 3.1. IPS face-to-face transactions pre and post creation of ChileAtiende

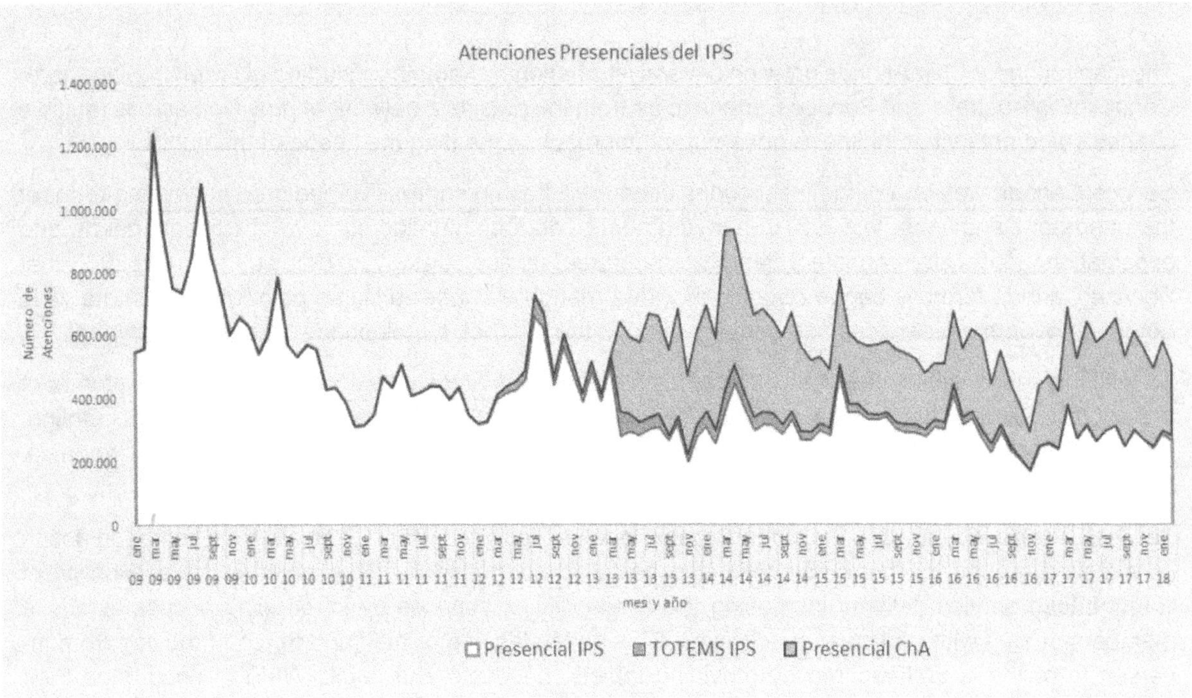

Source: Ministry of Finance (*Ministerio de Hacienda*) (2018[3]), *Presentación Nueva Institucionalidad ChileAtiende*

ChileAtiende itself was the result of bringing existing service delivery channels under a common brand but not common ownership. Face-to-face and telephone services were based on the longstanding service delivery model of IPS but the digital channel (initially the website and later expanded to social media and self-service kiosks) was commissioned by MDGU. Nevertheless, building on these established channels made it possible to take a more evolutionary approach. The IPS network represented an existing network of locations, providing a trusted source of access to the government across the country and with existing human, financial and physical resources to develop. The IPS network also had existing relationships with the National Health Fund (*Fondo Nacional de Salud*, FONASA) which reflected the intention of creating a unified service experience across the public sector.

Reflecting this patchwork approach, both the strategy and governance of ChileAtiende has been until recently split in two. The mandate of the President, MDGU and the Ministry General Secretariat of the Presidency (*Ministerio Secretaría General de la Presidencia,* MINSEGPRES) were responsible for the governance and political coordination for the network with its operation directed by IPS (see Figure 3.2).

Figure 3.2. Organisational Coordination for ChileAtiende

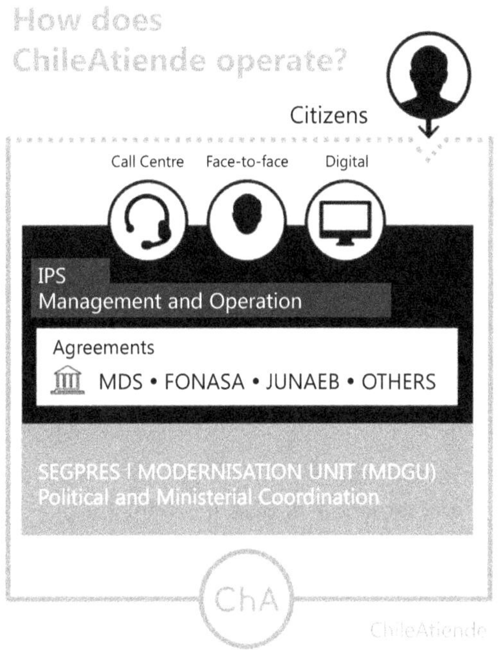

Source: Laboratorio de Gobierno (2016[4]), *La nueva relación entre Estado y ciudadanos a través de ChileAtiende*

The ChileAtiende Committee worked with the agencies to identify the most appropriate additional services to incorporate into the newly created ChileAtiende network. Although a mandate existed for creating ChileAtiende, there was no compulsion for the public sector organisations to include their services and so an approach was developed to encourage them to work with the new platform. Their approach to including services within ChileAtiende was three-fold:

1. First, identify the most heavily used services by citizens and businesses
2. Then, analyse those most heavily used services to identify other, related, services to add
3. Finally, increase coverage for services from small organisations with low levels of capability to develop solutions themselves

During this period, the government invested heavily in marketing with television campaigns running from 2011 to 2013 resulting in a suggested 30% increase in awareness and access of ChileAtiende. Having initiated this process and begun to work with public sector organisations to increase the quantity of services provided through the nascent ChileAtiende model, the priority became longer-term sustainability. Legislation was put to the Chilean Congress by the end of 2013 with the intent of establishing a standalone agency hosted at the Ministry of Finance (responsible for several public administration functions such as civil service, procurement and budgeting), with responsibility for the multi-channel service design and delivery agenda (Cámara de Diputados, 2013[5]). The Congress did not pass this legislation during this period.

The elections of 2014 returned former President Bachelet to office. Her previous period in power (from 2006 to 2010) had witnessed the creation of *ChileClick* and other e-government efforts as well as the pension reforms that affected the demand of IPS services and in doing so created spare capacity and the opportunity to develop ChileAtiende. Her term saw a shift away from central coordination to more localised decision making with public sector organisations delivering value according to their understanding of the needs of their users. As a result, there was no longer oversight and influence provided by the governance model that had been in place through the ChileAtiende Committee. Instead, efforts to leverage the

ChileAtiende digital channel were channelled through the Modernisation of the Public Sector Programme (Ministry of Finance) and DGD, which ran a project to increase the number of transactions in ChileAtiende's web channel for the period 2016-2019.

Moreover, due to the ChileAtiende brand being heavily associated with the Piñera Presidency there was also reduced enthusiasm within the new administration. Between 2014 and 2018, ChileAtiende enjoyed a lower profile with the IPS branding being re-emphasised and a more organisation specific approach becoming the priority. Although several institutions maintained the service focus of the ChileAtiende vision, some of the momentum to grow a cross-government, single purpose access point for citizens was lost.

Chile returned to the polls in December 2017 and re-elected President Piñera for a second term. In returning to power, he made ChileAtiende the flagship for service delivery. A key priority in his manifesto was to digitalise at least 80% of public procedures before 2022, aiming at having a "no queues and paperless" State by 2025. In pursuit of this, there have been efforts to de-politicise ChileAtiende by passing legislation that would institutionalise ChileAtiende and establish it in its own right and insulate it from any political upheaval.

This legislation is identical to that previously sent by President Piñera to Parliament at the end of 2013 (Cámara de Diputados, 2013[5]). It is intended to give the Ministry of Finance two responsibilities. First, responsibility for the vision of shared service delivery across the whole of government. Second, oversight and responsibility for delivery of the ChileAtiende network instead of IPS. The intention is to enshrine both ChileAtiende and the service delivery ambition in law to provide a sustainable approach to multi-channel service delivery that persists from one administration to the next. However, this discussion has not been prioritised in Parliament, with no progress during the period of this study.

Current approach to services in Chile

Oversight of services in Chile

Under the current administration in Chile, there has been steady support given to the modernisation and digital government agenda. The Government of Chile has worked with the OECD in developing several pieces of work to guide and shape the transformation of the public sector to take full advantage of digital government practices.

Digital Government in Chile: Strengthening the Institutional and Governance Framework (OECD, 2016[6]), delivered policy recommendations that guided subsequent reforms to the institutional framework for digital government in Chile in the creation of the Digital Government Division (DGD) in MINSEGPRES. This represents a step forward as now digital government is, by law, a public function performed by MINSEGPRES. As a follow up to this, *Digital Government in Chile - Making the Digital Transformation Sustainable and Long-lasting,* focused on embedding digital opportunities into everyday public sector operations in a whole-of-government approach.

The priority given to this agenda is reflective of the importance placed on the modernisation of the Chilean public sector. As a result, President Piñera has established a new institutional architecture to coordinate and lead modernisation of the State efforts (see Figure 3.3).

Figure 3.3. Institutional Architecture for the Modernisation of the State in Chile

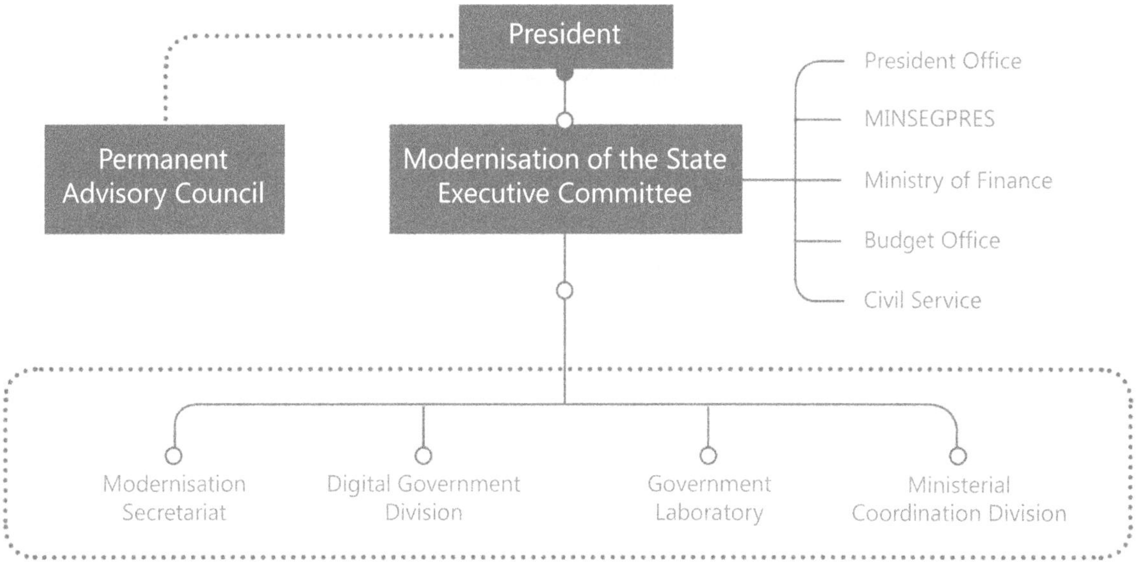

Source: Gobierno de Chile, (2019[7]), *Agenda de Modernización del Estado*

One of the most critical contributors to this is the Permanent Advisory Council for the Modernisation of the State. This council is appointed with an advisory role to the President on matters concerning both policy and also the machinery and organisation of government in areas such as public employment, budgeting and the digital transformation of the public sector, among others. This is quite a broad remit, and extends beyond the delivery of services and ChileAtiende.

The Council is a permanent body that meets every 15 days with a membership of 13 people consisting of representatives from academia, the private sector and those with a history of working within government. The members of the Council are appointed by government but are independent, following the model set elsewhere in Chile by the Council for Productivity in terms of a partial refresh of the membership every year.

The members of the Council see themselves as facilitators, especially where the topic has potential political sensitivity and this is helped by their apolitical status. Whilst the government sets the agenda, the Council is designed to help and improve what that agenda says in terms of how the government takes it forward, giving larger attention to the policies which have higher impact on the performance of the State.

The Council represents the perspective of those outside government and is complemented by the Executive Committee for the Modernisation of the State consisting of representation from the Office of the President, the Ministry of Finance and its Budget Office (DIPRES), the DGD of MINSEGPRES as well as the Chilean Civil Service. The make-up of this committee helps to achieve co-ordination by aligning finance with policy and delivery.

Through the Committee, four taskforces have been established to lead the modernisation agenda. First, the Modernisation Secretariat at the Ministry of Finance (former Modernisation of the Public Sector Programme) responsible for coordinating different cross-sectoral projects and exerting technical support to both the Council and the Committee. Second, DGD in MINSEGPRES responsible for digital transformation and data policies. Third, the Government Laboratory (*Laboratorio de Gobierno,* LabGob) providing focused consultancy to public agencies in terms of service design. Fourth, a co-ordination division within MINSEGPRES with oversight of government programmes and commitments that cut across organisations.

This Committee provides the high-level coordination and direction for the overall modernisation of the State agenda in Chile, including ChileAtiende. It is through their deliberations that the proposed legislation for institutionalising ChileAtiende is being reintroduced to the Chilean Parliament. Furthermore, this Committee has provided the foundation for the development of the Government's Digital Transformation Strategy (Box 3.2) making provision for several critical elements in the service design and delivery agenda for Chile and setting out the ambition for the future digital transformation of the country. This strategy has set specific goals for public agencies to achieve in terms of digitalising public processes, which form the basis for "no queues and paperless" mandate in the country.

One of the key milestones for the modernisation of the State in Chile is the recently passed Digital Transformation of the State Law (MINSEGPRES, 2019[8]). Among several other mandates, this law may represent a shift in public service delivery as it requests public agencies (both at central and local levels) to only use electronic means to provide services (paperless approach), stressing the relevant role for DGD in defining and implementing sound and coherent data sharing, digital identity and advance electronic signature strategies. The implementation of this law, within a timeframe of five years, presents a unique and significant window of opportunity for public agencies to not only simplify or digitalise products and services but create public value by transforming how public services can adopt a user-driven approach in rethinking public services.

Box 3.2. Chile's Digital Transformation Strategy and Digital Transformation of the State Law

The Digital Transformation Strategy

President Piñera has placed the digital transformation of the State at the core of his administration. DGD, the agency responsible for digital government, has defined a strategy for 2018 to 2022 which aims at having a paperless and no queues public administration (*Cero Papel* and *Cero Filas*). The ambition is for public agencies to digitalise public service delivery so Chilean people can benefit from digital technologies to ease their interactions with government. The strategy is driven by three aims:

- Better services for citizens and businesses, in order to increase public trust and well-being through timely and accessible services
- Better public policies, transparency and accountability through the strategic and intensive use of data as well as increased spaces for citizens participation
- Consolidated digital transformation of the State, as a long-term and permanent approach

The strategy sets out strategic and operational principles to be implemented. Additionally, the strategy establishes the operational needs for implementing the Digital Transformation of the State Law and the standards and technologies under the responsibility of DGD it requires (see below).

The Digital Transformation of the State Law

President Piñera promulgated the Digital Transformation of the State Law in November 2019 in order to provide the means for public agencies to deliver on the promise of simplifying interactions between citizen and State. The law mandates public agencies (both at central and local levels) to become paperless within five years, leaving paper-based procedures only for exceptional cases. The law requests that:

- all administrative procedures will be digital-based and stored in digital records;
- communications among public agencies will only occur through digital means;
- documentation requested for administrative procedures will need to be digital-based, and in case of paper-based documents these will need to be digitalised;
- administrative procedures will be signed using electronic signature;
- all notifications from public agencies to citizens will occur through digital systems and e-mails

There are five years before it fully enters into force but a single year in which to define a regulatory framework of standards and identifying platforms to equip public agencies. As digital by default becomes the standard for administrative procedures, the law will require a series of enablers such as:

- full interoperability between public agencies
- the consolidation of a national catalogue of services
- document management systems and standards (including strengthening the role of the National Archive in preserving official documents issued by public agencies)
- the expansion and strengthening of ClaveÚnica as digital identity system
- advance electronic signature mechanisms

DGD and the Modernisation Secretariats are responsible for coordinating and overseeing the production of these standards as well as for the compliance to the law before coming into force.

Source: Own elaboration based on División de Gobierno Digital, (2019[9]), *Digital Government Strategy* and MINSEGPRES, (2019[8]), *Digital Transformation of the State Law.*

The operation of ChileAtiende

Responsibility for ChileAtiende

Whilst the Council and the Committee provide high-level oversight for the modernisation agenda, including both digital government and service design and delivery, there is a dedicated Committee for ChileAtiende. This Committee comprises representatives from the Presidency, DGD, the Budget Office, IPS and ChileAtiende, and monitors the specific strategy and operation of ChileAtiende. The operational responsibility for operating ChileAtiende today rests with IPS with all of those who work for ChileAtiende being employees of IPS.

As of today, the operation of the entire multichannel network relies on IPS and its ChileAtiende division. Face-to-face and telephone channels have been under its responsibility since the creation of ChileAtiende but the digital channel (web and self-service kiosks) only recently transferred from the DGD of MINSEGPRES. Involvement of DGD in ChileAtiende now focuses only on developing guidance in terms of technology and the provision of particular enabling technologies, such as ClaveÚnica, Chile's digital identity solution (discussed in Chapter 4) and interoperability systems.

IPS has created an internal unit to lead on digital transformation rather than to draw on the resources and expertise of DGD. However, as their mandate is on the internal transformation of IPS rather than with a broader mandate to work with service delivery organisations across government it is anticipated that DGD will continue to develop the services and software required to support ChileAtiende, which may demand further clarification of roles.

Overall, government services in Chile operate independently and have to use a service specific platform. In the absence of a common service infrastructure, DGD manages PISEE (*Plataforma Integrada de Servicios Electrónicos del Estado)*, a SOAP-based integrated interoperability platform which provides data exchange only for a number of Chilean services. Figures from DGD indicate that only around 18% of interoperability agreements between public agencies occur through PISEE in 2019.

Channel strategy[1]

The channel strategy for ChileAtiende is three fold: multi-service, multi-channel, and multi-layer.

By being **multi-service**, ChileAtiende sees services aggregated from 28 institutions with a total of 274 services available for use (167 from IPS and 107 from other organisations). The quantity of IPS services provided through ChileAtiende reflects the close historic relationship between the two and those services account for 50% of all requests with 22% being related to health care and access to FONASA.

In being **multi-channel**, services are provided across face to face, telephone and digital (including website, social networks and self-service kiosks):

- **Face to face:** there are 254 physical locations where ChileAtiende can be accessed, with 192 of those permanent locations and the remainder accessed periodically by a mobile venue. In total, this provides 80% coverage of the country. A private provider puts on events for those without CA locations. 15% of these locations are shared with other service providers including the police, and the Service of civil registration and ID (*Servicio de Registro Civil e Identificación*, SRCel). 39 are designed to be inclusive spaces, offering spaces for breastfeeding and entertaining children as well as offering translation services by video call.
- The face-to-face channel is staffed by 1 500 officials and handles 6 million requests a year. This figure has dropped from a peak of 8 million visits in 2014. Many of those who use the face-to-face channel are unable to access services online.

- **Telephone:** the call centre of 65 operators receives 150 000 calls a month. All of these enquiries are for information rather than as transactions due to current limitations of the country's digital identity solution (see Chapter 4). Although many of the enquiries can be addressed by the team, a proportion of them are re-routed to the relevant provider elsewhere in government.
- **Digital:** the digital channel comprises the website, social media and self-service kiosks channels. The website receives 24 million interactions a year however, the current limitations of the country's digital identity solution mean that it is not possible to complete a transaction so these can only be for information. The social media team respond to 300 requests a day. Reflecting the increasing attention being paid to the digital channel the website is experiencing 30% year of year growth. The ChileAtiende website is a hub that hands off to services provided through the websites of the relevant organisation. The content for those websites, and ChileAtiende itself, takes place at the institutional level meaning that multiple sites must be maintained and there are challenges in tracking user journeys and performance. Some services have been developed for self-service kiosks; as these use a separate technical architecture to those services available online they could be defined as an additional channel.

Finally, in being **multi-layer**, services are provided according to the depth of integration with a given institution. For a number of services, and in all three channels, users can fully complete an enquiry or transaction with the relevant party but as highlighted, the constraints with digital identity mean more common experience is to provide information and then signpost a user elsewhere to carry out the necessary final interaction with the relevant service through the provider's own, separate, channel. Only services provided by FONASA can be paid for.

Currently, only 6% of the total number of public service transactions in Chile are offered directly through ChileAtiende meaning the vast majority of service interactions take place directly between a user and the relevant service provider's website, call centre or physical location (Ministerio de Hacienda, 2018[3]). Although ChileAtiende accounts for a small proportion of the total transactions carried out between the Chilean government and the public it reports a 71.5% satisfaction rating, which is the highest of all service providers[2].

Other service delivery channels[3]

With ChileAtiende accounting for a small proportion of all transactions between citizens and the state, an important part of understanding service design and delivery in Chile is how alternative channels manifest themselves. One of the biggest drivers for standalone services is the desire for different parts of government to trace their users. As a result, there are several different 'My account' services provided by organisations including ChileAtiende, FONASA and IPS amongst others.

In several cases, ChileAtiende lists the transactions and services offered by other parts of the government. Ongoing efforts to make ChileAtiende the preferential entry point for citizens in accessing public services are led by the Presidency, while for some agencies the ambition is that the separate bespoke channel would be replaced by working increasingly closely with ChileAtiende.

*Service of civil registration and identity (*Servicio de Registro Civil e Identificación, *SRCel)*

The SRCel has the largest service delivery network in Chile, operating from more than 400 offices across the country. A small number of these are co-located with ChileAtiende. Their call centre receives 60 000 calls a month and 30 000 contacts a year online. The ChileAtiende call centre and website provide a seamless experience of access SRCel services.

The SRCel falls under the remit of the Ministry of Justice and is responsible for managing 23 base registers including those dealing with identity, births, vehicles and drivers. The SRCel provides the underlying identity infrastructure for Chile's physical identity card the *Cédula de Identidad* as well as working with the DGD of MINSEGPRES on the digital identity solution ClaveÚnica.

As well as maintaining registers, the SRCel also issues certificates with around 13 million issued in persona and 19 million issued online each year. All certificates are available through the ChileAtiende website (as well as their own). The most popular certificate is one related to police records, which is needed when looking for a job. An integration for this data is provided to the Attorney General's Office but no other services are using it despite the frequency with which it is requested.

Certain services provided by the SRCel require the presence of a notary and as a result, there is a legal requirement for SRCel to offer a face-to-face channel. This is one reason why SRCel transactions are not all available at ChileAtiende locations.

Internal Revenue Service (Servicio de Impuestos Internos, SII)

The SII has 60 branches around the country and through their web channel alone handle 200 million transactions a year. 95% of those transactions are dealt with by first layer support agents.

SII's integration with ChileAtiende works in two ways. First, with the ChileAtiende call centre providing direct, first layer support to citizens for a certain amount of enquiries and routing them on to SII contacts where appropriate. Second, the ChileAtiende website contains information about 80 transactions. This information is duplicated on the SII's own website.

National Health Fund (Fondo Nacional de Salud, FONASA)

FONASA provides universal health coverage with private providers and counts 80% of the Chilean population (14 million people) amongst its users. Those on low incomes do not pay a fee whilst others pay 7% of their monthly income to access the health insurance and the level of care they access varies depends on the level of that payment. Citizens have the option of accessing private health providers if they pay a top up. It is expected that FONASA services such as certificates and sick leave approval status can be available through ChileAtiende in the near future.

It operates its own network of face-to-face service locations, a telephone call centre and a website. However, there are integrations with ChileAtiende locations in order for citizens to obtain the certificates and vouchers that are required to demonstrate eligibility or proof of payment. 80% of all transactions relating to healthcare insurance take place in person.

Superintendence of Social Security (Superintendencia de Seguridad Social, SUSESO)

SUSESO operates their own physical location with 74% of all claims made in person with a call centre that is able to provide information but no transactions. The other 26% of transactions are handled online, reflecting the low digital confidence of their users. SUSESO are eager to be absorbed into ChileAtiende do not want digital transformation to mean simply that some more digital certificates are available online, they view the potential of digital transformation via ChileAtiende to mean the creation of a universal platform that can respond to the unique challenges of any existing, or newly developed service.

Directorate of Labour (Dirección del Trabajo, DT)

DT operates from its own locations with 50 staff members attending to 750 000 calls year. It is the intention for ChileAtiende to provide a first layer of support in resolving simple, standardised procedures and, in time, for all procedures to be handled directly by ChileAtiende, at least over the phone. However, previous attempts at equipping ChileAtiende call centre staff to handle DT enquiries proved unsuccessful with the enquiries still being routed to DT.

DT has a commitment to developing services that focus on the needs of the user, ensure integration is possible and look to simplify interactions. However, many of their services are still paper based and so a technical platform is under development to create an omni-channel experience for their users. Whilst they would like to collaborate more extensively with their partnering organisations there was clear frustration that they had been unable to achieve an integration with FONASA despite their services accounting for 70% of DT's activity and such an integration having benefits on both sides.

Ministry of Social Development and Family (Ministerio de Desarrollo Social y Familia)

The Ministry operates its own call centre and website as well as a channel for written correspondence (both email and postal). The services it provides are included in the ChileAtiende website. In this case, a strong multi-channel approach has been developed with municipal governments with various services being made available through locations across Chile's 350 municipal governments.

Having integrated with the ChileAtiende call centre (in terms of enquiries being re-routed) the ambition is that the relationship between the Ministry and ChileAtiende would develop along the same lines as the provision of municipal governments and see requests for information and transactions handled by ChileAtiende.

National Consumer Service (Servicio Nacional del Consumidor, SERNAC)

SERNAC operates its own call centre, 16 physical locations and website (including a chatbot and click to call functionality). In addition to their own physical locations, they have co-located offices with 200 municipalities and are increasing their coverage through an alliance with ChileAtiende.

The nature of the service SERNAC provides (in providing support to consumers) means that the organisation is aware of the importance of putting users at the heart of what they do to ensure their needs are met. As such, their ambition is that it should not matter which channel is used or the provider so long as the necessary information can be exchanged to simplify the eventual outcome.

Like the Ministry of Social Development and Family, SERNAC has developed strong working relationships with municipal governments and encouraging them to adopt a consumer focus to their efforts in order to bring services closer to the citizen. It is better for everyone if the municipalities are able to resolve issues as close to where the citizen is based as possible.

350+ municipal governments

Although the Ministry of Social Development and Family and SERNAC have developed mechanisms for providing services through municipal government the local and regional service delivery experience is not one that has been the focus of the ChileAtiende project other than to highlight that each municipality provides a local face to face, telephone and sometimes also web based approach to accessing services.

References

Cámara de Diputados (2013), *Establece un sistema de atención a las personas y Crea el Servicio Nacional de Atención Ciudadana, Chileatiende.*, https://www.camara.cl/pley/pley_detalle.aspx?prmID=9536&prmBL=9125-06. [5]

Canada.ca (2019), *Improving services for Canadians*, https://www.canada.ca/en/employment-social-development/corporate/portfolio/service-canada/improving-services.html. [2]

Canada.ca (2019), *Service Canada Programs and Services*, https://www.canada.ca/en/employment-social-development/corporate/portfolio/service-canada/programs.html. [1]

División de Gobierno Digital (2019), *Estrategia de Transformación Digital del Estado.* [9]

Gobierno de Chile (2019), *Agenda de Modernización del Estado.* [7]

Laboratorio de Gobierno (2016), *La nueva relación entre Estado y ciudadanos a través de ChileAtiende.* [4]

Ministerio de Hacienda (2018), *Presentación Nueva Institucionalidad ChileAtiende.* [3]

MINSEGPRES (2019), *Ley 21.180 de Transformación Digital del Estado*, https://www.leychile.cl/Navegar?idNorma=1138479 (accessed on 12 December 2019). [8]

OECD (2016), *Digital Government in Chile: Strengthening the Institutional and Governance Framework*, OECD Digital Government Studies, OECD Publishing, Paris, https://dx.doi.org/10.1787/9789264258013-en. [6]

Notes

[1] Figures throughout this section are unpublished but provided during the OECD mission to Chile in January 2019.

[2] This is according to an independent citizen satisfaction assessment that is used to gauge satisfaction with 80% of all citizen services.

[3] Figures throughout this section are unpublished but provided during the OECD mission to Chile in January 2019.

4 An analysis of service design and delivery in Chile

This final chapter applies the conceptual framework described in Chapter 2 to the situation in Chile.

After an initial analysis of the context for services in Chile the chapter explores the philosophy underpinning this area of government activity. It does this through a discussion of service design and delivery leadership; the challenge of setting out the vision for a new channel strategy; the behaviours of service design and delivery and finally an overview of how service design and delivery in manifesting amongst particular organisations in Chile. The final section of this chapter is devoted to exploring the enablers to support services in Chile. It looks at the role of the Digital Government Division; the approach to standards and guidelines; the use of assurance processes and procurement; digital inclusion; the channel strategy; common components and tools; the opportunities associated with a data-driven public sector; and finally, public sector talent and skills.

The previous chapter provided an overview of the origins of ChileAtiende and a descriptive overview of service design and delivery in Chile. This chapter will apply the OECD analytical framework presented and explored in Chapter 2 to the experience of Chile.

The analysis will initially centre on the contextual situation in Chile. The second part of the chapter will then look at the philosophy of service design and the approach to delivery before the chapter concludes with an analysis of the different enablers to support service design and delivery in Chile.

Analysing the context for services in Chile

The ability for a country to respond to the opportunities of these approaches is heavily influenced by factors relating to society, technology, the functioning of government and existing legal frameworks.

There is high demand for face-to-face service delivery in Chile because of the demographics and geography of the country. Whilst user choice means up to 80% of interactions with FONASA take place in person there is a strong defence of face to face interactions as seen by the reaction when IPS proposed no longer paying the pension in cash to the 10% of recipients who prefer to receive it that way. The strength of reaction was such that the plans were abandoned.

For the team behind ChileAtiende and other service delivery initiatives the desire to achieve 'channel shift' onto digital and telephone channels is not simply down to the efficiency of the state, it is estimated that citizens spend 12m CLP annually on travelling to access face to face services. Face to face services are not only preferred by those who are digitally excluded through age and access to technology but more than one participant in the peer review indicated that literacy of the population was a barrier to providing online services. In this context the advent of voice assistants who cannot only understand spoken commands but return answers to questions become significant. There would be advantages to Chile considering how they might develop their services to reflect those possibilities.

However, lack of promotion and awareness of online services are also perceived as key barriers for the adoption of digital services. Indeed, digitalisation of services without adoption and literacy campaigns can end up increasing digital inequality and "empowering the already empowered". This also reflects on the need for having a dedicated strategy for digital services rationalisation, who oversees not only the national services offer but also which specific mechanisms are needed to expand their coverage and use.

The need for a more strategic understanding of the services landscape in Chile benefits from the recent development of the national catalogue or register of services (*Registro Nacional de Trámites*). This catalogue can help in developing a strategic approach to the migration, rationalisation or consolidation of those services that share similar characteristics. In the past, DGD of MINSEGPRES has attempted to maintain a limited record for only a fraction of the services. Keeping it up to date has proven highly challenging while different definitions of services, transactions and processes throughout the public sector, plus the law introducing its own definitions, mean no two 'services' may be alike.

Consolidating the catalogue or register of services paves the way for the possibility for the simplification and rationalisation of government by bringing together the various parts involved in administering the end to end experience of a user. A citizen may find themselves needing to complete one transaction with department a before having to tackle a further interaction with department b and possibly then returning to department a. An index of services therefore provides a tool with which to understand and map user journeys. It is positive that the Digital Transformation of the State Law (MINSEGPRES, 2019[1]) and its related regulatory framework mandate public agencies to register all their services in this catalogue. However, further efforts and institutional capacities are needed to ensure the strategic use of this catalogue in the rationalisation of services and the overall expansion strategy of ChileAtiende.

However, there are no maps of the data flows from one service to another. As a result, there is a gap in terms of understanding how frequently a given service is delivered or accessed. Whilst there have been relatively successful efforts to develop a cross-government analytics solution that can demonstrate 80% of all journeys, these are only for web transactions[1].

One of the most important aspects of transforming the experience of services is acknowledging and responding to the challenges of the long tail of government services. The original prioritisation criteria for ChileAtiende focused at one end on those services for which there was existing high levels of usage and at the other on those that belonged to smaller, less capable organisations. In general, those public sector organisations where services are high profile will have invested some effort in implementing a digital service of sorts but the tens or hundreds of low level paper transactions that may receive only a few hundred submissions a month collectively contribute significant overheads of time and energy for public servants and duplicated effort for citizens or businesses.

Procurement activity can also prove to be significantly constraining with one procurement cycle relating to the SRCel contract for both identity systems and hardware for face-to-face locations being out of synchronisation with the procurement activity for digital design and delivery. This procurement exercise was a three or four year process and at the end of which a ten year contract is being considered. Such long-term and painstaking procurement is a significant blocker to embracing an agile, twenty first century approach to the delivery of public services. This has the result of locking into place a model of delivery for one of the several face-to-face delivery networks that cannot be addressed for several years.

Chile's legalistic culture means that the focus and the priority is often on implementing legislation as the solution to a particular issue. As a result, the legal basis for a given service may prove to be overly prescriptive and require a political process to alter. Such a model is clearly a huge barrier to agile and iterative development of policy and services in response to a deeper understanding of the needs of a particular set of users.

This behaviour can be seen relatively clearly in respect of the approach to data sharing agreements within the Chilean public sector which are reported as taking a considerable length of time, potentially even to the point of abandoning the request and duplicating the data collection instead. In Chile, data sharing between agencies occurs through bilateral agreements given the required compliance to data protection regulation (MINSEGPRES, 1999[2]). While aiming at protecting citizens' privacy, this framework acts as a barrier rather than an enabler for data sharing: legal terms for data sharing may be discussed between agencies for years before being signed. Efforts to facilitate data sharing while ensuring ethical and trustworthy use of data should be at the core of the new data protection regulation in discussion, for example, empowering citizens to give consent and monitor data usage between public agencies. The OECD's concept of a data driven public sector recognises the importance of establishing a solid and effective data governance model to underpin and ensure a coherent and sensible approach to the role of data. One of the important aspects of this work is the mechanism that exists for one part of government to make use of the data held and controlled by another whether through technical solutions or the removal of any legal obstacles (OECD, 2019[3]).

The evolution of ChileAtiende over the course of its existence has also shaped the way in which other organisations relate to it and the stated ambition for creating a simple mechanism for citizens to access government services. Some public sector organisations view ChileAtiende as a no or low cost way of growing their own institutional coverage rather than an endorsement of ChileAtiende and a prelude to migrating from their own platforms. This exacerbates and perpetuates the duplication and fragmentation of channels.

Nevertheless, ChileAtiende remains an effective means for public sector organisations to reach more people through a highly regarded channel that is especially powerful in amplifying and catalysing the delivery of smaller organisations who probably do not enjoy the funding or capacity found in larger organisations. As such, the existing base of ChileAtiende provides an excellent opportunity to address the 'long tail' of government services (those that are low in volume and low in profile but which collectively cause overheads for both citizens and public organisations)

Moreover, there is clearly value in the ChileAtiende brand in terms of reputation amongst the public, and pride within its own staff. There is the potential for this brand to become a government-wide signifier of reliable, familiar and high quality services. However, any value in identifying this as a single brand is diminished by a proliferation of other channels with inconsistent design or delivery models mentioned earlier. This last point is one of the most pressing in the context of adopting an omni-channel service approach in Chile.

Analysing the philosophy of services in Chile

As discussed in Chapter 1 and Chapter 2, the philosophy of service design reflects an aspiration that is not the e-government approach of putting existing processes onto the internet but is a transformative approach to delivering public value that reflects the full experience of digital government.

Chile has demonstrated a commitment to unlocking the potential for digital government in transforming outcomes for citizens by establishing a sound governance framework, developing a sustainable ambition for the future and addressing the priority need for digital identity (OECD, 2016[4]; OECD, 2019[5]; OECD, 2019[6]). Combined, these provide the foundations for maintaining Chile's position as a regional leader in digital government. They are also valuable in creating the suitable conditions for building a culture of proactive, digital by design, open by default, user-driven services that benefit from both Government as a Platform and Data-driven public sector thinking.

This section of the chapter will consider the ways in which the experience of Chile discussed in Chapter 3 can be seen to reflect the philosophy of service design and delivery in terms of the behaviours and cultures shaping the delivery outcomes in the country.

Leadership

ChileAtiende is stated as one of the pillars of President Piñera's strategy for the digital transformation of Chile. The key ambition of this agenda is to bring public services closer to citizens. In order to achieve this it is necessary to simplify interactions between citizen and state, embed service design in the operational activity of the public sector and to maximise digital tools and practices. Building on the visible strategic leadership from the President, making such activity real requires strong, clear, ongoing leadership and a vision for the future across all public sector organisations.

However, the lack of cross-sectoral support for ChileAtiende legislation in the Congress brings the need to work collaboratively in order to demonstrate, and anticipate, the benefits of adopting a service design and delivery approach such as ChileAtiende promises to deliver. More work is required to embed a service design and delivery agenda at the very highest levels of the government in order to support the Congress in moving away from creating laws that specify the establishment of new services, platforms, registers and systems. This also means that alternative approaches to institutionalise ChileAtiende need to be considered beyond the approval of this legislation. For example, by strengthening the institutional role of IPS – and not solely ChileAtiende – in service delivery standards. Additionally, increased coordination, collaboration and integration between key incumbents in digital transformation and service design (such as DGD, LabGob, IPS and Modernisation Secretariat) and public agencies is needed in order to embed cross-sectoral service design and delivery principles in the implementation of the Digital Transformation of the State Law (MINSEGPRES, 2019[1]).

ChileAtiende is currently into its third political administration and it is clear that the shifting political context has a bearing on the approach to service design and delivery in the country. Whilst the brand of ChileAtiende is strong and has high levels of awareness amongst the public this reflects a challenge because of how closely identified it is with President Piñera. During the administration of Bachelet this association appears to have resulted in the deprioritisation of cross-government service provision whilst President Piñera's return to office has clearly seen a greater priority given to it once again.

It is unfortunate for this agenda to have become politicised, as there is value in having a clear and coherent strategy for delivering services in Chile, particularly in the context of several competing channels that are leading to confusion and overheads of time and energy for citizens and operational cost for the government. Nevertheless, there is an excellent opportunity to capitalise on two things. First, the fact that the President has the desire to provide significant political backing. Second, that ChileAtiende appears to be universally endorsed with everybody understanding that it is a good initiative. This should allow for an ambitious agenda of setting standards, showing leadership and creating momentum.

This is particularly true in helping embed the practice and culture of cross-government service delivery and reduce the reliance of this agenda on political will. The ambition to use legislation to set ChileAtiende on a more secure footing is a valid one. However, there is a tendency to look to the law as a solution that will automatically address the issues. Progressing with the legislation to bring ChileAtiende under the responsibility of the Ministry of Finance may well be transformative but there is no guarantee that this will succeed and so different approaches may be needed.

Therefore, creating the conditions to join-up efforts across institutions and create a sense of common contribution to, and ownership of, a common cross-government service agenda will be helpful in depoliticising such an important initiative. This is pivotal for raising awareness and recognition of the relevance of *ChileAtiende* for the State, not for a single government. There have already been some important steps that have been taken to support the institutionalisation of service design and delivery approaches in developing a platform approach to service design and delivery.

The creation of the Permanent Council for the Modernisation of the State is an important initiative in terms of bringing together key actors to discuss ongoing activities and address some of the continuity issues. It is particularly important that this Council has been created in a way that means it will persist into a subsequent administration and is therefore less susceptible to the shifting priorities of a different political leader. ChileAtiende is seen as an important element in the infrastructure of state to achieve modernisation and continuity of delivery, especially during periods of crisis. It is one of key initiatives under the pillar Better Services for Citizens (*Mejores Servicios para las Personas*) in the Modernisation Agenda of President Piñera. However, there was less evidence of an ambition for how it might underpin the transformation of the state through a comprehensive and coherent rationalisation of service provision in Chile.

Furthermore, the support to the Council by the Committee for the Modernisation of the State includes important representation from the Presidency, the Ministry of Finance (in terms of financing future development) and the DGD of MINSEGPRES (in terms of delivering the digital transformation agenda). However, this lacks the presence of IPS and the representation of cross-government service delivery at the highest level. It is essential that the service delivery agenda is able to receive the leadership and mandate for challenging some of the existing divergent behaviours.

Under the stewardship of IPS, ChileAtiende has become exceptional in delivering an operationally effective and highly satisfying experience for its users. However, their responsibility has not yet extended to setting the strategy or developing the vision for the future of cross-government service provision or the mandate to define what good looks like. Whether this change is brought about through legislation or not, a capability for leading the cross-government service agenda is necessary. As such, the ChileAtiende and IPS design and delivery leadership should be viewed as integral to the future of a government wide service design agenda. This is demonstrated by the Service Council that meets every month and which defines government services and sets their expectations on what good looks like.

There is certainly a need to increase the frequency, quality and effectiveness of service design and delivery related communication and collaborative decision making between public institutions and the government to support better outcomes and encourage collaboration and integration. This indicates that the multi-disciplinary nature of the team leading the service design agenda needs to include diplomatic influencers as much as those with visionary delivery skills.

In the event that such delivery cannot be centrally mandated, it will become even more important to set a clear and compelling vision for the role that ChileAtiende can play as a platform for service delivery. Collaborating with parts of government building strong networks that are mutually beneficial will become essential if the leadership is lacking to be able to compel the migration of services from bespoke, organisation channels into a genuinely shared single access point to government. In this context the existing roles of the Ministry of Finance in controlling spend and the DGD of MINSEGPRES in establishing the standards for digital delivery become important as levers to shape outcomes for service delivery.

The experience of the Directorate of Labour (*Dirección del Trabajo*, DT) is perhaps instructive in identifying how service design and delivery leadership can be implemented without resorting to laws and coercion. DT has demonstrated a strong focus on responding to the needs of citizens, not through introducing a new team or set of practices to the organisation but through top-level leadership committing to this agenda. The Ministry of Finance and MINSEGPRES could consider exploring similar approaches to create the momentum throughout the Chilean public sector. A network and culture of digital leadership helps propagate different ways of thinking and working and can draw out the potential of those across government and within an organisation from senior roles to the most junior.

It is imperative that a model is identified that can embed service design and delivery leadership throughout the Chilean public sector in order to avoid the potential for the agenda to be neglected following any change in political leadership. The service design and delivery agenda should not ebb and flow according to politics but maintain a relentless focus on meeting the needs of citizens at all times in pursuit of a more effective and efficient state.

One of the potential mechanisms for supporting this is the innovation leadership displayed by the LabGob (Box 4.1). The potential for joint working between IPS, LabGob and DGD can make an important contribution to leading and shaping the behaviour and delivery of public servants across Chile. It is critical that these two organisations identify ways to work with strategic alignment that contributes to the sustainable, embedded transformation of service design and delivery culture across the government.

Box 4.1. Government Laboratory (*Laboratorio de Gobierno,* LabGob)

Founded in 2014 as the first Latin American Government Laboratory, LabGob is focused on articulating a new relationship between the State and its people. It represents a new approach for Chile in addressing public challenges by placing people at the centre of government activities to create and implement solutions that deliver value. It does this in two particular ways:

- An agile and flexible consulting service that promotes the co-design of solutions that are tested and validated for a public problem through joint work of specific service teams and LabGob.
- The Public Innovators Network: a movement of public officials, civil society organisations, members of the academy and students and anyone sharing the objective of improving the quality of services that the State provides.

LabGob's value proposition of improving services provided to the public is built around five principles:

1. Focus on people: shifting the focus from "things" to one centred on people, in order to understand their needs, assets, motivations and capacities as agents of the innovation process.
2. Co-creation: to complement the focus on people, co-creation is the way LabGob understands active collaboration. It consists of opening spaces, delivering tools and motivating multiple actors to co-discover, co-define, co-devise and co-implement innovations that have impact.
3. Systemic approach: integrating multiple perspectives through a holistic look at problems and solutions. Inter and tran-sectoral coordination and the use of systemic thinking allow LabGob to break down disciplinary and management silos to govern complexity.
4. Experimentation: this is how LabGob develops its solutions and learns about its processes. By building prototypes and taking a "learn by doing" approach, practical knowledge is built that informs, improves and makes possible the solutions while discarding bad ideas and strengthening good ones.
5. Focus on the experience: LabGob proposes new ways of understanding and communicating, based on stories and visual thinking. It provides an experience of innovation from a space, identity and materiality that helps to make training in public innovation a tool of culture change.

Source: Laboratorio de Gobierno, (n.d.[7]), *El lab*

Setting a vision for a new omni-channel strategy

The ChileAtiende brand is strong, not only in terms of its name but in its visual identity and the sense of pride expressed by its staff. This is an important factor in supporting the original vision for ChileAtiende: it is valuable for governments to be focused on simplifying the ease with which citizens can access the state and to live up to ever increasing expectations through the agile, iterative development of services that places users at their heart and are driven by their needs. This will deliver not just more efficient government but higher quality services that take advantage of all the opportunities provided by digital government approaches.

The challenge for those interested in the future of ChileAtiende is to refresh that vision and the pitch for 2020 and beyond to focus on achieving an exciting ambition for the future that addresses some of the challenges facing the service design and delivery agenda in Chile, particularly in light of the COVID-19 pandemic and given the patchwork of service delivery. Whilst ChileAtiende may be a well-regarded and all-encompassing service delivery brand it is simply one of several brands relating to departmental and public sector organisation delivery with the result that there are a myriad of competing channels meaning duplicated effort for government and a fragmented and disorienting user experience for the public.

Any power in committing to ChileAtiende as the single brand is diminished when it acts as an index of things with signposts off to websites or physical locations owned and branded by others. Other public sector organisations in Chile view cooperation with ChileAtiende as a way of growing their own coverage and achieving their own ambitions rather than as an endorsement of ChileAtiende. The simplicity and minimal additional costs of including their services means that they experience no additional friction in maintaining their duplicate channel and do not view cooperation as a prelude to migrating away from it.

Therefore, at the centre of any future vision for ChileAtiende or services in Chile there must be a commitment to radically rationalise and consolidate existing service delivery channels through greater partnership working and a commitment to collaboration. ChileAtiende should be encouraged by the example of SERNAC and the Ministry of Social Development and Family who have developed effective partnerships with municipal and regional government and shown that there is potential for collocating services alongside multiple providers.

It is important that those with the authority have the vision for ChileAtiende to become the single visual brand under which Chileans complete their interactions with the state. This means that some existing attitudes may need to be revisited and incentives provided for them to change. For example, the government wants to see more services provided under the umbrella of ChileAtiende but at the same time calls on other existing channels to reflect the same level of quality experienced at ChileAtiende; these are confused and contradictory and perhaps reflect a reluctance to prioritise the necessary closure and consolidation of other channels. Instead, as well as securing the necessary capabilities to expand the services provided through ChileAtiende there needs to be budget, incentives and leadership to accelerate the migration from these fragmented channels to a single front door from the perspective of the user.

This is a critical point. ChileAtiende and IPS are at their best when focused on customer service, not in attempting to hold the responsibility for designing and delivering services for every organisation within the Chilean public sector. The delivery of those services in the first place is best handled by the organisations who are responsible for particular users and their needs. The brand of ChileAtiende will be most effectively supported by changing the underlying culture across the Chilean public sector so that the 'single front door' provides access to reliable, familiar, quality services that may look like they are delivered by a single entity but which continue to be the responsibility of each organisation. However, there is here an opportunity to bring together IPS (ChileAtiende), DGD and LabGob to define the end to end standards (customer service, strategic use of digital and service design respectively) that equip public agencies in implementing the law as well as to enable the provision of these transactional services through the ChileAtiende network. Bringing the 3 actors together would consolidate institutional understanding of their users needs, awareness of their preferences and the adoption of innovative approaches.

This needs to be approached from both the perspective of the large, self-sufficient organisations such as SII and SRCeI but it should also be considered from the perspective of those smaller organisations that have already shown that such an approach can work such as DT, the Ministry of Social Development and Family or SERNAC. Not every public sector organisation is going to be as receptive to the involvement of the Centre of Government. The bigger agencies will not want to lose the direct relationships with their users whilst the small ones are glad to take advantage of an existing network because it amplifies their work. ChileAtiende has the potential to be a powerful platform for the medium and small volume services that may otherwise be stuck with paper interactions.

Beyond the vision for offering a genuine single service delivery brand the vision for services themselves is similarly in need of a refresh. One of the important characteristics of service design is the idea of establishing an end to end view of the user's experience and understanding how their journey moves between channels and potentially interacts with multiple organisations. Such an understanding requires a recognition of the importance of back office integration and the possibilities for transforming a service rather than simply digitising a process. At the moment, many organisations are content being part of a single point of access rather than pushing the boundaries of a broader transformation.

Behaviours of service design and delivery

Having established the necessary leadership for service delivery and a vision for the outcome in question, the behaviours and culture of service design and delivery are critical. Service provision by Chilean public sector organisations is currently most often experienced and delivered through a paper-based and siloed model with most interactions between Chileans and the State requiring the exchange of documents and certificates. The pivotal role of paper is in part due to public sector organisations having been mandated by law to create dossiers for providing and processing public services (MINSEGPRES, 2003[8]). However, the Digital Transformation of the State Law (MINSEGPRES, 2019[1]) requires public sector organisations to transition to the provision of electronic dossiers and document management systems. Whilst the ambition for no queues and paperless government is to be welcomed, this mandate risks simply digitising existing bureaucracy rather than rethinking whether existing services, practices, procedures and culture meet the needs of users or exploring opportunities to work across government.

The modernisation process is not simply about having services on the internet that better meet the need of citizens and other stakeholders; it is also about transforming the underlying way in which government responds to the needs of citizens. This is well demonstrated by the design of ChileAtiende locations to be as inclusive as possible with sign language interpretation available and special spaces for breastfeeding mothers. The institution of ChileAtiende prides itself on coming as close to the user as possible and this is borne out by the high levels of satisfaction that the face-to-face service receives.

Perhaps the greatest asset that ChileAtiende has is its staff. The men and women who provide the face-to-face care understand how important their role is in triaging the issue somebody is facing, understanding how to support them and providing them with the necessary care. The atmosphere within the ChileAtiende locations is welcoming and friendly which puts people at ease and allows them to engage in a positive fashion, regardless of how upset or agitated they might be. It would be relevant to identify the specific attributes of face-to-face service delivery in order to embed them as foundational values and principles for the entire network.

As a result, there is a priority in Chile for retaining the physical environment for providing services. Around the world, several countries have pursued efficiencies by closing and reducing the face-to-face infrastructure only to find that their attempts to establish a "digital by default" environment has caused distress to their stakeholders and simply created greater demand through other, more expensive channels.

This strong commitment to customer service and the experience of users in the built environment can now provide the basis for Chile to consider transforming the experience across the public sector of what is currently quite a fragmented and disjointed user experience. The ambition for ChileAtiende was to provide a common front door through which to access government services. Whilst the experience of some services through ChileAtiende are seamless, the challenges with digital identity for validating users over the telephone or online limits the extent to which people can get their issues resolved as quickly as they might like. Whilst the fact only 6% of government services can be accessed through ChileAtiende mean it is highly likely that citizens will end up needing to access a service provided elsewhere in government. As a result, the transformation of service delivery in Chile will not occur if data are not valued and a clear and coherent strategy developed (OECD, 2019[3]).

Nevertheless, there are opportunities for ChileAtiende, IPS and the other service delivery organisations in Chile to do more in the context of bringing citizens into the discussions about the design and delivery of services. The conversations held during the research visit to Santiago in January 2019 did not surface many references to participatory forms of need analysis or user research. The first and second principles of the *Recommendation of the Council on Digital Government Strategies* (OECD, 2014[9]) underline the importance of engaging citizens, businesses and civil society through crowdsourcing and collecting their input in the design of digital government strategies and their related policies. The ChileAtiende network provides an excellent resource for hosting user research sessions but also for working with other local providers to develop a cross-government understanding of the experiences citizens have. A partnership between ChileAtiende, and DGD would likely prove valuable in exploring this possibility and help develop cross-government ownership for the needs of the public. In addition to this, ChileAtiende would benefit from exploring similar arrangements for studying customer experience as well as incorporating the work LabGob carries out in public service design.

Whilst the physical network of ChileAtiende locations provides a suitable venue and opportunity for collaboration there are other opportunities that a truly transformed approach to designing and delivery government services might unlock. One of these is the fact every government department has a complaints and suggestion officer; these individuals have insight into where government services are going wrong, and where they're going well but they do not currently work together to coordinate across channels and understand the interactions between different parts of government.

The human opportunity for joining up professions across government provides the basis for developing service communities of policymakers, service designers, software engineers, and operational staff to break out of organisational siloes and understand how to better meet the needs of users. An interesting example in this direction is "Clase Media Protegida" from the Ministry of Social Development and Family, which comprises several services from different public agencies under the concept of providing security networks to middle class families. This project has required increased coordination between different agencies in order to provide a consistent and coherent user experience and offers a model for what cross-government delivery might look like. However, it has created another network and a further brand around service delivery that perpetuates some of the confusion about channels which will be discussed later. Moreover, there remain technical challenges for Chile in the integration challenges when it comes to existing back office systems.

In the effort to continue improving services one of the most important behaviours of service design and delivery is measuring the impact of what's delivered and learning from how a service is being used. These efforts to understand performance should move away from simplistic measurements towards a more comprehensive and standardised model for gathering insight. The Modernisation Secretariat (former Modernisation of the Public Sector Programme) has been working since 2016 in defining a cross-sectoral and standardised methodology for measuring citizens' satisfaction, as described in Box 4.2.

Box 4.2. Citizen satisfaction survey

Since 2015, the Modernisation Secretariat of the Ministry of Finance has focused on increasing the efficiency and efficacy of public institutions as well as citizen satisfaction with public service delivery in Chile. The Secretariat (formerly the Modernisation of the Public Sector Programme) has collaborated with the Inter-American Development Bank (IDB) to fund modernisation projects for key Chilean public institutions, setting specific KPIs in citizen satisfaction to measure the degree of impact and success of the initial ten projects.

In order to assess these projects as well as to facilitate comparative analysis, the Secretariat developed a standardised yet adaptable methodology and survey to capture how satisfied citizens are with the products and services these institutions deliver. Along with providing net and gross satisfaction rates, the survey characterises types of users, channels and products and services. It also determines which specific institutional and/or service delivery attributes have a significant impact on citizens' experience with public services, serving as a powerful tool for high-level officials and policy makers in addressing to what extent service delivery is truly responding to citizens' needs in Chile.

While each Chilean public agency conducts its own citizen satisfaction measurement, a common methodology has been agreed to facilitate comparative and longitudinal analysis while providing strategic insights for service delivery policy making. As of today, and with the endorsement of the Budget Office, the survey has increased its scope, comprising 29 public institutions and covering around 80% of total demand for service delivery in the country (not including health and education services). Institutions are measured every second year, reaching a total of 81.500 surveys conducted to date to capture citizens' perception with face-to-face, digital and/or telephone channels. The methodology, related studies and results in both data visualisations and open data are available at https://satisfaccion.gob.cl.

Source: Own elaboration based on Ministerio de Hacienda, (n.d.[10]), *Portal Satisfacción de Servicios Públicos*, https://satisfaccion.gob.cl

How particular organisations are demonstrating service design and delivery

Different parts of the Chilean public sector are making greater progress in terms of the involvement of the public, the adoption of user-centred design approaches or the iteration of services in response to performance insights. This section of the chapter will conclude with a brief description of the philosophy of service design and delivery in a selection of organisations.

*Service of Civil Registration and Identity (*Servicio de Registro Civil e Identificación, *SRCeI)*

The SRCeI handles the process by which births are registered. This team are considering the opportunities for service design in two ways. First, by locating SRCeI offices in 1% of hospitals to allow parents to complete the registration shortly after a baby has been delivered. Second, by exploring a pilot for a digital birth certificate.

Internal Revenue Service (Servicio de Impuestos Internos, SII)

SII has a team of over 800 people working on delivering services and independently considering the experience and journeys of its users. These teams are focused on changing the perception of taxpayers towards SII and that means these teams are not exploring cross-government service provision or deeper integration with ChileAtiende. They are focused on four discrete activities:

1. **Experience management**: developing an understanding of taxpayers in order to develop new technologies and services to meet their needs. The organisation previously had assumed it knew what taxpayers wanted but now a user-centred design methodology has revealed that they did not. This team works with development teams to carry out research and test new services.
1. **Long distance assistance**: this team is exploring new ways of meeting the needs of users who access services online including the testing of a chatbot. This team is responsible for the web content.
2. **More complex information**: this team is working to help taxpayers understand information. They do this through training programmes and providing responsive social media support in the channels where people are asking questions
3. **Operations department**: a technical team addressing some of the internal challenges with SII systems in order to help understand the full end to end lifecycle of a taxpayer's journey including the back office steps.

National Health Fund (Fondo Nacional de Salud, FONASA)

Whilst FONASA has implemented a business intelligence department to increase the capacity of the organisation to measure its impact and understand its value the approach towards service design and delivery was quite traditional. The organisation has an internal development capability but development takes place in a closed environment with the service only being opened up for users to access when the moment comes to implement the enhancement. FONASA would benefit from exploring agile ways of developing services that could allow them to rethink the way in which FONASA services operate, particularly in their exchange of information with healthcare providers as well as in the overall user experience.

Superintendence of Social Security (Superintendencia de Seguridad Social, SUSESO)

SUSESO are responsible for auditing and regulating social security. They also manage public funds and are responsible for distributing information about social benefits. The administrative system for SUSESO is electronic from end to end. When people make a complaint it is filed electronically, the fil is analysed electronically and then the process is completed using the advanced electronic signature. Companies and people are informed electronically. Their model contains four elements:

- A predictive model that's used to identify who's coming to make a claim
- An integrated data model
- Connected to 20 different systems and 600 other services
- Connected to 60 other institutions so they can collect information from them

Directorate of Labour (Dirección del Trabajo, DT)

DT has adopted a very progressive attitude towards service design and delivery with an approach that sees digitalisation as the inevitable consequence of a focus on the user, a commitment to integration and simplification of processes. This is exemplified by their commitment to an "omni-channel" approach. In understanding their users' access to technology they recognised that there is no point in putting a service online if it misses the intended audience.

As a result, they have developed some valuable examples:

- The channel by which a user chooses to access a service does not matter. If they only get part way through it they will be able to use any other channel to pick the transaction up again.

- Online services can be access through a face-to-face interaction with a customer service agent providing training and building the confidence of the user to access the service themselves.
- Their data integrations with 600 institutions allows them to automatically pay an allowance to families with low incomes without their having to apply.

Analysing the enablers to support services in Chile

Creating the conditions in which reliable and high quality services can be designed and delivered is the combination of three separate areas of focus. First, as discussed at the start of this chapter, the context in which services are being developed. Second, the philosophy that has been adopted by a country towards the delivery of services. Third, and finally, the enablers to support services.

This report is considering the experience of service design and delivery in the context of Chile, informed by the experiences of other OECD member and non-member countries around the world. Chile has an opportunity to take advantage of the country's strong track record in providing multi-channel services to use the ChileAtiende network to establish a single service brand that might create a more coherent and cohesive experience for citizens and government. This is not to say there should be a single entity called ChileAtiende tasked with designing and delivering every single service in Chile but that there is a possibility to develop a consistency of design, a simplicity of messaging and a confidence of usability that follows from the existing ChileAtiende approach. Unifying the service experience of citizens in Chile could deliver a step-change in simplifying the relationship between citizen and state and meeting the needs of citizens more effectively.

For such an approach to work, services developed to fall within the experience of ChileAtiende will require the provision of enablers that support coherent service delivery. This support for services can come in various forms as discussed in more detail in Chapter 2 under a Government as a Platform approach that equips public servants to deliver services. These enablers meet the needs of service teams in the work of researching, designing and implementing a given approach but also speak to the challenges of adoption and ensuring that the public experience the benefits as fully as possible.

First, this section will discuss the role of the Digital Government Division (DGD) within the Ministry General Secretariat of the Presidency (*Ministerio Secretaría General de la Presidencia,* MINSEGPRES) and its influence as Chile's Digital Government Unit and lead contributor to developing the enablers that underpin the design and delivery of transformed services.

The role of the Digital Government Division

As discussed previously it is important for the government to be clear about its vision for ChileAtiende. If the decision is to pursue a single brand with a clear expectation for creating a consistent user experience then this requires establishing clear assurance mechanisms and the necessary support for teams across government to adopt a new way of working. In taking this agenda forward, the team at ChileAtiende has the right attitude towards delivery that puts citizens at the heart and can spread that enthusiasm for meeting needs. However, in order for ChileAtiende to be successful, it requires the underlying services to go through a similar transformation and in this respect, the DGD of MINSEGPRES becomes increasingly important.

The creation of the DGD within MINSEGPRES was indicative of the higher political standing and additional resources being provided to the digital government agenda following the publication of Digital Government in Chile (OECD, 2016[4]). The influence of DGD has further benefited from the participation of the Head of the DGD in the Committee for the Modernisation of the State ensuring visibility of the development of digital government efforts across Chile. As discussed previously in this chapter, it may prove valuable for IPS and

ChileAtiende to be represented in that Committee in order to give the necessary priority and attention to cross-government multi-channel service design and delivery.

DGD has been delivering strongly against the digital government agenda in Chile and has been instrumental in bringing about the three recent pieces of documentation that underpin the digital transformation, and service design and delivery, agendas. The Presidential Instructive on the Digital Transformation of the State Administration (Presidente de la República, 2019[11]), the recently passed Digital Transformation of the State Law (MINSEGPRES, 2019[1]) and a renewed Digital Transformation Strategy for the Government (MINSEGPRES, 2019[12]) collectively reinforce the mandate of the DGD. That mandate provides for DGD to set standards for delivery, deliver tools, provide resources, offer consultancy and monitor the progress and compliance of the Digital Transformation Plans throughout government. In addition to those assurance and governance functions, the documents set out the priority for developing the "Zero Queues" (*"Cero Filas")* approach for simplifying processes, the "Paperless Policy" (*"Cero Papel"*) for removing paper, the importance of ClaveÚnica for digital identity and a focus on establishing base registers.

Standards and guidelines

One of the important coordinating roles that the DGD plays is in defining standards and providing guidelines. Indeed, amongst the more ambitious for the service design and delivery agenda public sector organisations in Chile, there was an appetite and desire for DGD to be more exacting in the expectations placed on the quality of delivery and the mandate for particular behaviours to be enforced. With the Digital Transformation of the State Law passed at the Congress this is even more important, as DGD is mandated to define technical standards, guidelines and cross-cutting services which will equip public services to implement the law. The implementation of the law would benefit by embedding cross-sectoral standards for service design and delivery as part of the core principles for public agencies to transform their services.

The centre of government is well suited to the role of setting standards in having a clear view of cross-government priorities. The role of DGD in the Committee for the Modernisation of the State and the ongoing focus on the transformation of the government ensures that any standards are not based on assumptions but rooted in the shared priorities of the government. ChileAtiende is not the right vehicle to police the implementation of standards but alongside other delivery agencies, should form part of the collaborative process in identifying those service design and delivery standards and refining the assurance mechanism for encouraging a sustainable shift in the way that services are designed and delivered.

However, whilst there are currently no common standards or principles for the way in which services are designed and delivered there are several important resources under development by DGD. These include a software development guide for the State, an IT procurement guide, directives related to the use of cloud computing and a cloud technical guide, an open data guide and perhaps critically, the Digital Services Manual.

Moreover, there are some other central guidelines under the proviso of the "Zero Queues" (*"Cero Filas")* approach for simplifying processes and the "Paperless Policy" (*"Cero Papel"*) for removing paper from government services. There are sector specific initiatives such as with the SII who have implemented the standardised documentation of processes in order to identify opportunities for improvement but this is not a service design methodology.

Assurance processes and procurement

Key Recommendation no. 9 of the *OECD Recommendation of the Council on Digital Government Strategies* (OECD, 2014[9]) underlines the importance of using business cases to reinforce the digital policy of the public sector, contribute to improved planning, development, management and monitoring of investments in digital technologies. Paired with controls on spending above a particular threshold, these mechanisms can prove useful in coordinating public spending, avoiding duplicated (or wasted) effort and providing scrutiny to increase accountability and trust in government. In Chile, spend is not currently analysed at a national level or within each department and the spend controls process is an advisory exercise that is carried out on request rather than being a strategic and all-seeing exercise in coordinating spend.

Although the Ministry of Finance and DGD have done some analysis of what has been bought and what has been spent in terms of software licences and outsourcing procurement remains an area where there are opportunities to introduce greater scrutiny of digital and service related spending.

Although Chile has developed an online purchasing marketplace, *ChileCompra*, the vision for transforming procurement as an enabler for designing and delivering services is somewhat limited. Chile could learn from some of the examples discussed in Chapter 2 in terms of how governments have rethought and transformed procurement activities to open up the market to new suppliers, simplify and optimise the contracting process and focus on outcomes rather than on hourly rates whilst making contract data openly available as Open Government Data. With the increasing needs for the implementation of the Digital Transformation of the State Law (MINSEGPRES, 2019[1]), which implies redesigning and digitalising public service delivery in the country, developing a healthy supplier base for the agile design and delivery of services is particularly important given some of the skills constraints discussed earlier in this chapter. It is highly unlikely that the Chilean public sector will be able to recruit and train in sufficient quantities to meet demand and so the role of the private sector will be critical in achieving the country's digital government ambitions.

Currently procurement activity can block service transformation with issues relating to long-term contracts having expensive change control processes and little in the way of a framework model to derive best value for the Chilean taxpayer. *Digital Government in Chile - Making the Digital Transformation Sustainable and Long-lasting* (OECD, 2019[5]) made several recommendations to the Chilean government in terms of transforming procurement, and particularly the purchase and commissioning of digital and ICT services.

Digital Inclusion

The focus of this report is multi-channel service delivery in the recognition that for significant quantities of the Chilean population the face-to-face channel is preferable. Whilst Chile continues to explore how they might deliver high quality services through face-to-face channels there is nevertheless a desire to simplify, transform and digitise the interactions between citizen and state according to the principles of the digital government approach. The question of digital inclusion is has relevance to this discussion and can take the form of enhanced connectivity, increased digital literacy and questions of accessibility.

The principles of the OECD Recommendation of the Council on Digital Government Strategies (OECD, 2014[9])highlight the importance of establishing the digital skills and competencies throughout all segments of a population. The provision of government services through multiple channels, including face-to-face, rather than embracing a digital by default approach that could create potential digital divides is therefore an approach for which Chile should be praised.

Chile has relatively low levels of citizens using digital channels to engage with government services. Chile's National Survey of Socioeconomic Characterisation (Encuesta de Caracterización Socioeconómica Nacional, CASEN) found that 30.1% of the population used the internet to complete a government procedure over the last year (MIDESO, 2017[13]). This is despite Chile enjoying above Latin America and the Caribbean (LAC) and OECD averages in terms of the population share using the internet and having a mobile subscription per 100 people (see Figure 4.1). In the context of Chile's geography, these figures are quite an achievement and, combined with the data in Figure 4.2, indicate that perhaps Chilean society is skipping the fixed internet connectivity state to move more towards mobile access.

Figure 4.1. Proportion of internet users and mobile subscriptions in Chile compared with OECD and LAC countries, 2016

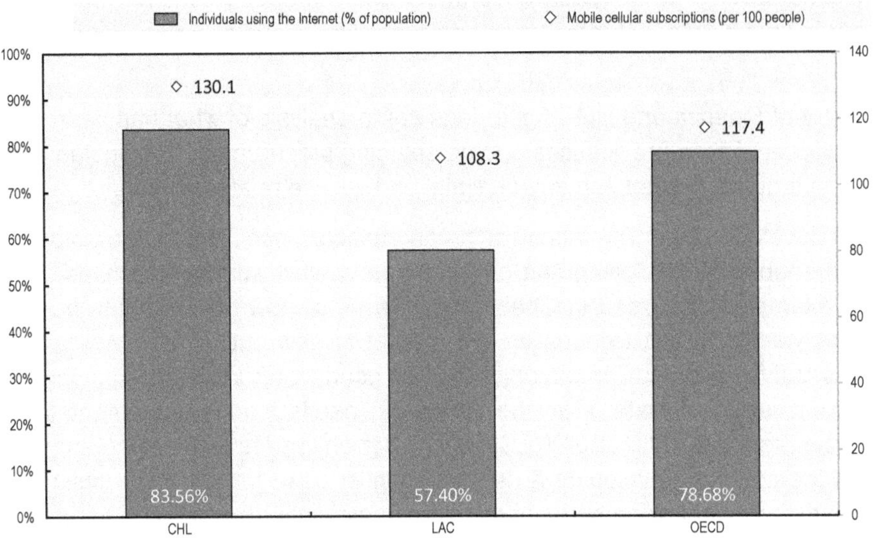

Source: World Bank (2016) World Development Indicators, https://datacatalog.worldbank.org/dataset/world-development-indicators

Figure 4.2. OECD fixed broadband subscriptions per 100 inhabitants, by technology, Dec 2017

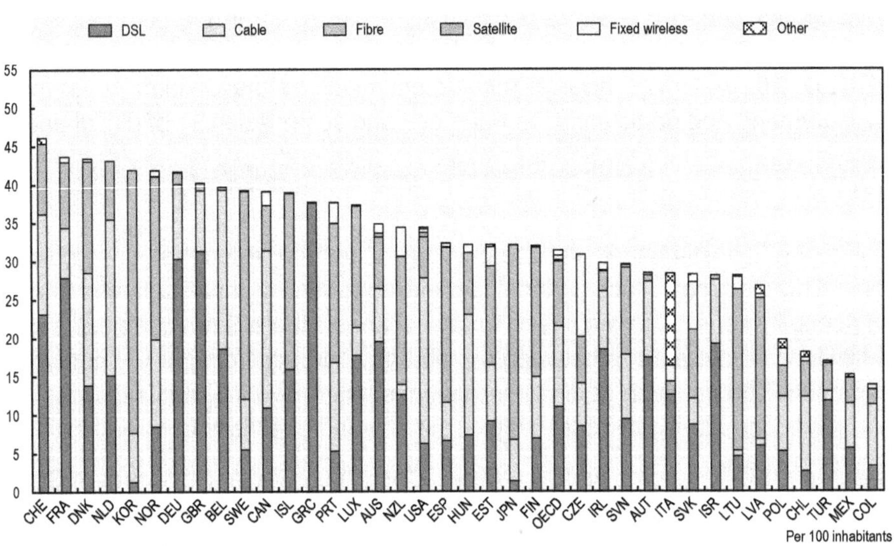

Notes: **Australia**: Data reported for December 2018 and onwards is being collected by a new entity using a different methodology. Figures reported from December 2018 comprise a series break and are incomparable with previous data for any broadband measures Australia reports to the OECD. The OECD definition of fibre differs substantially from fibre classifications commonly used in Australian reporting. These figures treat connections known in Australia as 'Fibre-to-the-Node' and 'Fibre-to-the-Curb' as DSL connections, while 'Fibre-to-the-Premises' and 'Fibre-to-the-Basement' are treated as Fibre connections. Data on technology type prior to Q2-2016 should be treated as indicative until further notice. **Canada**: Fixed wireless includes Satellite. **France**: Cable data includes VDSL2 and fixed 4G solutions. **Israel**: Data are OECD estimates (information on data for Israel: http://oe.cd/israel-disclaimer). **Italy**: Terrestrial fixed wireless data includes WiMax lines; Other includes vDSL services. **Mexico**: Access points are reported since operators cannot provide information of subscriptions by technology. Data for **Switzerland** and **United States** are preliminary.
Source: OECD, Broadband Portal, www.oecd.org/sti/broadband/oecdbroadbandportal.htm

In terms of explicit digital literacy activities, several of the service delivery networks, as well as ChileAtiende provide assistance to those who choose to access services face-to-face in terms of supporting them to learn and understand how they might use the internet to access government services. Elsewhere, the government has partnered with BancoEstado and Servipag to use the ChileAtiende network for providing financial education. With the physical ChileAtiende locations meeting the needs of the most vulnerable populations there are many possible opportunities to work with policymakers and other agencies to use the face-to-face setting as a valuable element in end to end service transformation in this way.

In 2019 Chile hosted several Asia-Pacific Economic Co-operation (APEC) meetings with one of the action points from that meeting for Chile to carry out a "Gap Assessment on Digital Literacy" to ensure continued progress on addressing the digital divide which prevents women from fully participating in trade. Such research could provide some important insights for how the service design and delivery agenda advances.

Channel strategy

In the context of ChileAtiende, the Government as a Platform ecosystem includes the website, call centre and face-to-face locations with their self-service kiosks. These enablers provide the support to the other relying partners in the Chilean public sector to put their services in front of the public and meet their needs. Currently the different channels under the ChileAtiende brand are not working together to deliver the same service as there are bespoke solutions being developed on a channel by channel basis. The website does not have the same architecture as the information available in the call centre, which in turn is not the same as what agents are using in the face-to-face locations or what is running on the kiosks. One of the priorities for ChileAtiende to have a coherent and unified user experience is that platforms themselves need to be designed according to the same principles as public facing services; the experience of public servants is important in maximising the transformative potential of service design and delivery.

When it comes to new services joining the ChileAtiende platform there should be an investment in time to simplify the onboarding of new services. The ChileAtiende and IPS teams should be committed to understanding the friction experienced by partner organisations choosing to start using the ChileAtiende platform. These teams should be resourced to ask themselves how to make it as simple, and effective, as possible to add a new service and to find ways of avoiding training and integration overheads. If every service that wants to use ChileAtiende channels needs experts at the ChileAtiende side then the model will be unsustainable. Instead, ChileAtiende needs to be developed in such a way that new services are made available without much fanfare and can be iterated and improved as easily as possible.

The value of the single government branding and a single place for content can prove incredibly powerful in transforming internal cultures and coordinating service delivery. Indexing different services that hand off to another website that duplicates some of the infrastructure or the administrative overhead is not as effective as developing a co-publishing model where responsibility for setting priorities, enforcing standards and managing some content is held at the centre but teams of editors are distributed throughout government with ownership of their particular subject area. Currently there are five individuals within ChileAtiende tasked with managing a vast amount of content whilst on the service provider side the people tasked with this activity are doing it on the margins on their job. The pressures on editorial staff are particularly pronounced if content continues to be housed in multiple websites.

Committing to a single service delivery brand also necessitates developing a single government domain to become the front door of content for many services. As a result, it is essential to resource content properly in order to recognise this aspect of the design of services as equally important to the technicalities of how the service works. With the implementation of the Digital Transformation of the State Law (MINSEGPRES, 2019[1]), this becomes critical as services should be designed and developed in order to be embedded and offered through ChileAtiende channels, strengthening a single and coherent service delivery policy in Chile. This is particularly true in a society such as Chile where low levels of literacy mean it is critical to find the simplest way of communicating as possible.

Common components and tools

The final area of analysis for the enablers to support service design and delivery in Chile are the technical platforms provided by the DGD for use and re-use by teams throughout the Chilean public sector. There are currently five relevant platforms with the DGD team continually investigating whether they might develop any more. One of the enabling resources that is currently lacking is related to taking payments. ChileAtiende does collect money from users wishing to pay for their FONASA fees but this is not possible over the telephone or for any services accessed via the Mobile ChileAtiende. In the absence of an integrated payment system, ChileAtiende will not be able to offer paid services from other public agencies such as FONASA. It would be relevant to see IPS, DGD and the Ministry of Finance coordinating the adoption of cross-sectoral payment standards to integrate these specific services.

Simple

A business process mapping and process management tool for helping public institutions automate and digitise procedures and processes in a friendly, quick and easy way. Simple puts tools for designing services into the hands of public servants and reducing some of the time and resource constraints on bringing new services online. Simple also provides process tracking to allow citizens to stay informed about the status of their enquiries. Simple represents a swift mechanism for making an existing process digital, and offering some scope for streamlining and rationalising it.

ClaveÚnica (Chile's Digital Identity)

Chile is at a transition in terms of its approach to DI. Having built on the existing model of demonstrating identity with a physical card, the country launched ClaveÚnica in 2012. This mechanism for proving that someone is who they claim to be when accessing online services is now moving into a further development to extend its functionality and utility with the ambition that it becomes the default mechanism for people to access, and grant permission for access, to their records across the public and private sector. The functionality of ClaveÚnica is intended to allow for:

1. Data authentication: the mechanism by which citizens will be identified to access state services and other private organisations
2. Data wallet: A store of personal data for citizens derived from automatic sharing of data among agencies, which will allow interoperation with institutions on the basis of the access and re-use permissions which a citizen grants on their information.
3. Advanced electronic signature: Users of ClaveÚnica will be able to sign electronic documents issued by public bodies
4. Citizen mailbox: A means by which the state will notify citizens of important information and progress on their interactions with the state
5. Web portal eID: a website where citizens can manage access to their data, grant and revoke permissions and update their personal data

Chile is currently exploring how ClaveÚnica might develop in future to support the next phase of the digital transformation of government. They recently worked with the OECD to produce a 13 country comparative study of digital identity (OECD, 2019[6]) which contained several recommendations about how to proceed.

Digital identity is a foundational enabler to the design and delivery of modern, twenty-first century services. Currently, ChileAtiende is only able to carry out transactional services with those who attend a face-to-face location as the reliability of identity is not sufficient for many online and every telephone based request that might be made. Its importance is demonstrated by the fact that multiple digital identity solutions are in place. In Chile, 40% of the nation's 3 542 procedures can be carried out online. Of those, 989 require an authentication mechanism. 122 use ClaveÚnica, 145 use ClaveÚnica alongside their own authentication system, and 722 use their own authentication system (OECD, 2019[6]).

In line with the recommendations of *Digital Government in Chile – Digital Identity* (OECD, 2019[6]), Chile still needs to strengthen ClaveÚnica if expectations are to transition to digital and paperless interactions between citizens and public sector organisations. This requires addressing existing governance discrepancies between DGD and SRCel, as well as to equip ClaveÚnica with the right security and scalability mechanisms (such as incorporating a second authentication factor). The absence of a coherent and strategic approach towards DI may put in risk existing efforts and implementation process for the Digital Transformation of the State Law (MINSEGPRES, 2019[1]).

The implementation of Digital Identity is critical as its absence is a barrier to basic channel shift and more advanced transformation efforts. However, the new vision for ClaveUnica is about more than just identity and imagines a critical component of transforming services, not just digitising processes. This extends to the opportunities for putting citizens in control of the access to, use, and re-use of their data through the data wallet; this mechanism reflects the importance increasingly being placed on the way in which handling data influences the trust of citizens in government (OECD, 2019[3]).

FirmaGob

The Advanced Electronic Signature is a set of technological tools available for institutions to self-manage the issuance and management of certificates for their own authorities or officials authorized by Ministers of Faith of each institution. Under the existing strategy for digital identity, ClaveUnica will replace FirmaGob by providing cloud-based advanced electronic signature (MINSEGPRES, 2019[12]).

Datos.gob.cl

Chile's Open Government Data website where the Chilean public sector publishes datasets to stimulate possible innovation in society or support citizens in scrutinising the government.

DocDigital

This allows any government institution to process documents that require a digital signature by authorities for either internal or external processes. It makes an integral contribution to the efforts associated with the "Paperless Policy" (*"Cero Papel"*) for removing paper from government services.

Data-driven public sector

The OECD's Data-driven public sector model, discussed in Chapter 2, identifies the importance of establishing a coherent and comprehensive data governance model, focusing the application of data for public value, and thinking about the role data can play in building, and damaging, trust in society.

Data governance

Data across each of these categories is an important consideration in the context of designing and delivering services. It is positive to see that the Digital Transformation Strategy for the Government (MINSEGPRES, 2019[12]) places an emphasis on being a "Government based on data" and committing to addressing some of the challenges which were identified in the analysis of Chile's approach to service design and delivery. One of the options that Chile could consider is establishing the role of Government Chief Data Officer (or a similar position with sufficient political and administrative influence) to take the lead responsibility for leading and stewarding the development of a national data strategy. Such a role could provide the Chilean public sector, and the public at large, with clarity about how Chile is approaching the topics of ethics, interoperability, access, availability, governance, analytics and others.

There have been efforts are efforts to establish something like the once only principle to prevent government from re-requesting information from users that it already holds. For certain services IPS doesn't re-request information and the complexity of some certificates has been reduced in order to allow for them to printed with a resulting reduction in the need for face to face interactions. In general, the impression that was given about data sharing access was that it did not flow smoothly or easily and there was almost no mention of Open Government Data (aside from some publicly available dashboards). Overall, public agencies did not want to share data and they had no incentives, nor mandates to do so.

The OECD's concept of a data driven public sector recognises the importance of establishing a solid and effective data governance model to underpin and ensure a coherent and sensible approach to the role of data. One of the important aspects of this work is the mechanism that exists for one part of government to make use of the data held and controlled by another whether through technical solutions or the removal of any legal and regulatory obstacles where appropriate. However, with a couple of notable examples, the level of integration across the Chilean public sector is still less effective than it might be with challenges in terms of identifying available data and significant barriers to the easy access or sharing of the data in terms of the process for coming to an agreement between two parties.

The recently passed Digital Transformation of the State Law (MINSEGPRES, 2019[1]) should help disrupt this scenario. The law and its associated regulatory frameworks should address the current issues in governing and sharing data across Chilean public agencies. However, evidence in Chile suggests that a law may not be sufficient to avoid requesting data to citizens that public agencies hold: the Law for Administrative Procedures (MINSEGPRES, 2003[8]) mandated this to public agencies since 16 years ago. In order to increase the effectiveness and ownership of this regulation, guidelines and standards should be developed under a collaborative and participatory approach, involving public agencies in their drafting and development.

Application for public value

There were some good examples of organisations that were creating public value through their use of data in delivering services:

- **FONASA** showed some data exchange was taking place. The health insurance service relies on the SRCel and uses the National ID card. Eligibility for health coverage is based on being checked against a database that is made available on a local basis according to catchment area.
- **SUSESO** had pursued data integrations with 600 institutions, including the SRCel. For a service dealing with time off from work due to medical reasons. SUSESO enters the name of the individual with part of their identifying credentials and get the information back. The process used to take 120 days to provide a solution to a problem but it is now 30. However, this integration highlights one of the broader challenges of developing ChileAtiende as a unifying service delivery platform as SUSESO faces the prospect of losing some of this integration in order to connect into ChileAtiende. ChileAtiende is causing their potential clients to carry out integration work rather than those efforts being on the ChileAtiende side.
- **The Ministry of Social Development and Family** is responsible for the calculation and targeting of welfare benefits. To do this they access data from the Social Register of Homes as well as 18 other databases in order to design and deliver policy. Whilst getting access to the data is possible, it was quite a challenging process.

Another way in which data can be applied to generate public value is through the evaluation and monitoring of government activity, policies and services. Within ChileAtiende's services, there are challenges of tracing the journey of a user from the ChileAtiende website on to one of the service providing websites and beyond. However, in the face-to-face channel, the use of the National ID card creates a situation where customer service agents have access to the history of the individual and can establish what services have been accessed and the status of those requests.

Trust

The ability for government to access the trace of your requests and their status can introduce concerns about the appropriateness of how your data are used and the question of consent. Legislation is currently being developed in Chile that would enhance the ownership people have in terms of their data and the ability to grant, or deny, permissions for it to be used. The intent of the law is to empower users in giving them control. This is related to the future vision and ambition for ClaveÚnica in the context of providing a digital identity solution. As the OECD recommends, data should be treated under ethical and trust principles to foster data-driven public sectors (OECD, 2019[3]). Chile would benefit if DGD implements the right mechanisms to ensure transparency and accountability in the use of personal data for public service delivery, for example by making data interactions available in a personal citizen folder – as it is expected to deliver through ClaveÚnica wallet.

These efforts should also contemplate the development of soft law and agile instruments addressing the ethical side of data access, sharing and use within the public sector. This, as a means to influence public officials' self-regulation, and promote a risk-based data culture that places trust and the generation of value for citizens at the core of the public sector ethos, in line with digital rights.

Public sector talent and skills

There is not currently a culture of service design and delivery skills in the Chilean public sector but there are signs of efforts to improve that and encouraging examples on an organisation-by-organisation basis. In addition, as highlighted previously, there is in general a lack of involvement from stakeholders, whether citizens or public agencies with some public servants speaking of the need to "educate users" to ensure they could successfully negotiate a government transaction.

In order to establish a service design and delivery culture it is important to have the necessary skills in both service design and technical delivery roles. However, various organisations in Chile reported that this is not the case. It was encouraging to hear from DT about their plans to not only invest in the skills of the public but to focus on developing internal skills too.

In general, annual employment plans from departments have a focus on the attitude of workers towards users. This approach is echoed by further education providers where the Diploma in Public Management focuses on giving tools to public managers to think of citizens as customers. These are important and valuable customer service activities but they lack the technical dimension of considering the needs for service design and delivery.

Chile faces a significant digital and design skills shortage and efforts are needed to recruit new, and train existing, talent across the public sector. One helpful development is the creation of the Digital Transformation Coordinators network. Under the mandate of DGD, this body congregates institutional delegates for monitoring the implementation of the Digital Transformation of the State Law (MINSEGPRES, 2019[1]), and may serve as a fruitful school for digital champions in Chilean public administration as well as a route to engage key stakeholders in what should be understood and owned as a cross-government agenda.

More substantively, the Civil Service and DGD have partnered to increase digital awareness among Chilean civil servants. The Digital Academy (*Academia Digital*) has been established to provide a general introduction to those who want to understand how new technologies can be adopted and used in public service delivery. However, these efforts are in their infancy with further development of the curriculum and sophistication of its modules required not only to increase awareness but to equip teams with the right digital skills. This is particularly critical given the timeline for implementation of the Digital Transformation of the State Law (MINSEGPRES, 2019[1]) and the expectations to move to a paperless administration in a timeframe of 5 years.

References

Laboratorio de Gobierno (n.d.), *El lab*, https://www.lab.gob.cl/el-lab/. [7]

MIDESO (2017), *Encuesta de Caracterización Socioeconómica Nacional*, Ministerio de Desarrollo Social de Chile. [13]

Ministerio de Hacienda (n.d.), *Portal Satisfacción de Servicios Públicos*, https://satisfaccion.gob.cl/. [10]

MINSEGPRES (2019), *Estrategia de Transformación Digital del Estado*, Ministerio Secretaría General de la Presidencia. [12]

MINSEGPRES (2019), *Ley 21.180 de Transformación Digital del Estado*, https://www.leychile.cl/Navegar?idNorma=1138479 (accessed on 12 December 2019). [1]

MINSEGPRES (2003), *Ley 19.880 que establece bases de los Procedimiento Administrativos que rigen los actos de los órganos de la Administración del Estado*, https://www.leychile.cl/Navegar?idNorma=210676 (accessed on 12 December 2019). [8]

MINSEGPRES (1999), *Ley 19.628 sobre Protección de la Vida Privada*, https://www.leychile.cl/Navegar?idNorma=141599&buscar=19628 (accessed on 12 December 2019). [2]

OECD (2019), *Digital Government in Chile – A Strategy to Enable Digital Transformation*, OECD Digital Government Studies, OECD Publishing, Paris, https://dx.doi.org/10.1787/f77157e4-en. [5]

OECD (2019), *Digital Government in Chile – Digital Identity*, OECD Digital Government Studies, OECD Publishing, Paris, https://dx.doi.org/10.1787/9ecba35e-en. [6]

OECD (2019), *The Path to Becoming a Data-Driven Public Sector*, OECD Digital Government Studies, OECD Publishing, Paris, https://dx.doi.org/10.1787/059814a7-en. [3]

OECD (2016), *Digital Government in Chile: Strengthening the Institutional and Governance Framework*, OECD Digital Government Studies, OECD Publishing, Paris, https://dx.doi.org/10.1787/9789264258013-en. [4]

OECD (2014), *Recommendation of the Council on Digital Government Strategies, OECD/LEGAL/0406*, OECD, Paris, https://legalinstruments.oecd.org/en/instruments/OECD-LEGAL-0406. [9]

Presidente de la República (2019), *Instructivo Presidencial sobre la Transformación Digital de los Órganos de la Administración del Estado*, Presidente de la República de Chile. [11]

Note

[1] Evidence provided during the OECD mission to Chile in January 2019.

www.ingramcontent.com/pod-product-compliance
Lightning Source LLC
LaVergne TN
LVHW081409110826
845149LV00010B/1678
9789264758605